Biddy White Lennon's
Leaving Home Cookbook

A Paperback Original
First published 1989 by
Poolbeg Press Ltd.
Knocksedan House,
Swords, Co. Dublin, Ireland.

ISBN 1 85371 061 X

Cover design by Pomphrey Associates
Typeset by Print-Forme,
62 Santry Close, Dublin 9.
Printed by The Guernsey Press Ltd.,
Vale, Guernsey, Channel Islands.

Biddy White Lennon's Leaving Home Cookbook

POOLBEG

Foreword

"Most of the world's great dishes were created by people who could not read and write."

Robert Crofty Cooke

Every year thousands of young people leave home for the first time to take up a job, go to college or to emigrate.

By no means the least disturbing change in your life will be the fact that, for the first time, you will be solely responsible for feeding yourself. Some of you will have prepared the odd meal at home, but never before will you have had to plan, budget, shop and cook for yourself.

You will be leaving a well-equipped, well-stocked home to live in a bed-sitter or shared flat with the use of a corner of a communal kitchen. The equipment available to you will be basic in the extreme, the storage facilities poor, and your budget small.

Of course you can always take the easy way out and rely for nourishment on fast-food shops, canteens, or processed ready-prepared foods. But if you do this you will be poorly nourished and even poorer in pocket.

This book offers you an alternative way, by setting out to prove that self-catering is simpler, cheaper and healthier. It assumes no previous knowledge or experience. All the recipes are based on serving one person, using limited equipment, on a low budget. It is dedicated to my son Dairsie, whose dire need forced me to sit down and write it all out for him.

Contents

Things to Cook

Introduction

Since the day that people discovered the fact that certain foods tasted better than others and that some of these foods tasted even better if they were heated in a fire, cookery has been part of human culture. Ages before people had any need or desire to read or write they had discovered the joys and comforts of good food. People got on quite well for a very long time without specialist cooks or, for that matter, cookery writers. The skills were learned, generation by generation, by watching what went on round the camp-fire just as they still are today in simple societies. We don't live in a simple society. The complexities of living in our society dictate that in any domestic unit most if not all of the cooking is left to one person and the other members rarely have time to observe or to take part in the purchase or preparation of what they eat. Education has been taken over by specialists who train other specialists. Only a very small minority study the craft of cooking.

It used to be much simpler. There was a restricted range of foodstuffs available and so it was easier to master the techniques of buying, storing and preparing them. Nowadays, with quick, easy transportation and refrigeration, people expect to be able to buy and eat a wide range of foods from every corner of the globe. This expectation has created a new breed of "cooks" called food manufacturers.

Food manufacturers declare that people no longer need to slave in a kitchen. They claim that they can do it for us. They claim that they can do it better, manufacturing food that is sanitised, pasteurised, stabilised, emulsified, colourised, pre-cooked, ready-to-heat and serve. To do this they first of all remove everything that makes the food unique, its shape, its taste, its colour, its texture, its essential nutrients; then they invent it all over again to fit into their tidy containers using moulds, chemicals, dyes, vitamin enrichers and taste enhancers. It's called "adding value." I believe it has gone too far.

People are now divided into two camps, those who demand that most of their food reaches them prepared and pre-cooked, needing only a quick blast of microwaves to heat it up, and those who still have a taste for REAL FOOD.

The very rich and the very poor still enjoy real food. If you are just setting out on an independent life you are unlikely to be in the first category. The very rich pay very skilled cooks to prepare for them the very best food. The very poor in third-world countries cannot afford to buy manufactured, value-added food and eat only staple foods grown locally and simply prepared in the traditional manner. Young people leaving home for the first time in our society are in a position to have the best of both worlds. They can buy locally grown foods and other foodstuffs from all over the world to cook simple, cheap and healthy meals. IF THEY KNOW HOW TO COOK.

This book is for you. There are no complicated recipes in this book. You do not have to be an expert to produce tasty, healthy meals quickly and cheaply. I know what you need to learn because my own son is about to leave home. He likes good food but hasn't a clue how to set about cooking it. This book assumes that you have never cooked anything for yourself before. I recommend that you read the first two sections and become familiar with the basic cooking methods and the terms used before attempting any of the recipes. To help you do this I have included a glossary of terms at the end of the "How to Cook" section. If some of the cooking instructions seem obvious just remember that one of the hardest things to cook just the way you like it is a boiled egg.

Things You Must Know

Basic Equipment

You will need

1 7-inch chef's knife

1 4-inch chef's knife

1 3-pint enamelled cast-iron pot with fitted lid

1 10-inch heavy non-stick cast-iron frying-pan with lid

1 7-inch lightweight frying-pan

1 heatproof glass measuring jug which is scaled to measure both fluid ounces and millilitres

1 set plastic measuring spoons

2 wooden spoons

1 heat-resistant plastic spatula

1 slotted spoon

1 potato masher

1 stainless steel strainer which fits into your 3-pint pot

1 hand whisk (non-metallic)

1 grater

1 large plastic funnel

1 pepper-mill grinder

Knives

Blunt knives cause accidents. They also make life very frustrating in the kitchen. You need two sharp knives. The 7-inch chef's knife can do almost anything you need in the kitchen. A smaller 4-inch blade is needed for peeling vegetables. Modern stainless steel looks marvellous but is almost impossible to keep sharp without access to an electric knife-sharpener. The old-fashioned iron blades can be sharpened with a cheap whet-stone or even a flat-bladed file. *Sabatier* make the knives used by many professional chefs.

Cooking-Pots

A multi-purpose pot that can be used on direct heat and in the oven is essential. It should have a tight-fitting lid and have no handles or knobs which can melt in the oven. Heavy enamelled cast-iron is the best choice, particularly if you can find one on which the enamel is not applied as a thin coating over the pot but is part of the metal. *Culinar* makes such a range. They are much easier to clean and the enamel coating cannot chip or crack. The 3-pint size is the best all-round pot but if you can manage a smaller "sauce" pot as well then you will be equipped for most tasks.

Frying-Pans

You need one which is heavy, thick-bottomed and, preferably, with a fitted lid. Enamelled iron is unsuitable as the high heat often used for frying can crack the enamel quite quickly. Plain, old-fashioned cast-iron pans are cheap to buy but difficult to keep and can react chemically with some vegetables. The best choice is a heavy iron pan coated with a thick, non-stick coating. A 10-inch pan will be suitable for most dishes but too large for omelettes and pancakes. If you get a smaller 7-inch pan exclusively for these it can be much lighter and cheaper.

Utensils

Nothing destroys enamels or non-stick pan surfaces quicker than scraping them with metal. Cheap plastic can melt in seconds and does not improve the flavour of food. Old-fashioned wooden spoons are indispensable but must be kept scrupulously clean.

Buy a good-sized flat spatula designed to be used with non-stick pans. They withstand heat better than the cheaper types. A slotted spoon is needed for lifting food out of hot liquid or fat. The stainless steel strainer will be used for straining water from

6

food but also for steaming food. This is why you should choose one which fits inside your main cooking pot with the lid in place. You can get them with adjustable metal leaves and a central lifting stem.

You will need a whisk for making sauces. Get one made from wood or hard plastic so that you can use it without damaging your pots.

The perfect grater, like the perfect pot, has yet to be invented. Metal graters stay sharp but soon discolour and rust unless you clean them and dry them very carefully. I still prefer these old-fashioned, square, metal ones because they are easier on the knuckles. Plastic graters are never sharp enough.

The plastic funnel is essential for straining frying fats back into their container after they have cooled.

A set of plastic measuring spoons on a ring will be graded from a quarter-teaspoon to half-a-cup and cost buttons.

Christmas, Birthday and Leaving-Home Presents
There are a thousand-and-one gadgets on sale which claim to make the life of a cook easier and safer. Most of them do—at a price which is well beyond the pocket of the just-left-home cook. There are one or two which should definitely go on a list to be passed round to well-got relatives and tearful grandparents who might like to make your life-without-mother that bit pleasanter.

Dutch Oven
When I left home at eighteen and set up my first kitchen I fought my way through the next January sale and bought a small electric frying-pan cum oven—sometimes called a Dutch-oven. It has been in daily use for twenty years and my son is looking at it today with an acquisitive gleam in his eyes. It is quite simply the most useful thing I have ever bought. I use it to fry, bake, slow-roast, braise, keep food warm, heat serving-dishes, and

even as a fancy table-top cooker. It uses a mere fraction of the energy of a full-sized cooker and is perfectly suited to cooking for one or two people. This would definitely be the first item on my list.

Mouli-Sieve
This ancient piece of equipment has been superseded by the food-processor. But for a few pounds it can tackle many of the tasks of that much costlier piece of equipment. It runs on elbow-grease which is much cheaper than electricity. Get the largest size which can hook firmly over a big bowl.

Food Processor
Without question this is the next most useful small electric kitchen appliance. As time goes by and you become an experienced cook you will want one and, when you get it, wonder how you ever did without it. It should be on your list before a toaster, a deep-fat fryer, a cake-mixer, a pressure-cooker, a coffee-percolator or a microwave oven.

Mortar and Pestle
Indispensable for crushing and grinding whole spices and preparing pastes. Buy a good Italian stone one rather than the cheaper wooden ones which tend to crack and splinter.

Weights, Measures and Oven Temperatures

No system for classifying the weight of ingredients, the volume of liquids or the small amounts of seasonings or spices needed to prepare a particular dish, is perfect or even used consistently or universally.

When Mrs. Beeton issued her classic instruction for Yorkshire pudding "take a dozen eggs," she omitted to mention whether she meant small, medium or large eggs and she had never heard of Class A, B or C eggs. How big is a clove of garlic? What weight of cheese will fill a cup when it is grated? What on earth is a slow oven? Is a gas cooker quicker over a hundred metres than an electric oven?

The measures used in cookery books vary. They can be based on the old British Imperial measures, the European metric system or the American system of "cup" measures. No single system is perfect.

A system based on weight is as accurate as the scales and the care with which they are used. It can be extremely tedious to have to weigh out every tiny amount even if the scales are accurate enough to allow it. In my experience home kitchen scales are never accurate below 4 ounces.

The American system is quick and convenient, requiring only a scaled measuring jug and a set of standard spoon-measures. But it is not particularly accurate when measuring dry ingredients like flour. Because most dry goods have a different weight for the same volume, it can be difficult to visualise the correct amounts when you must purchase them by weight.

Most food writers use a combination of all three methods, not out of perversity, but because it makes life easier in the end. They will use weights where the ingredient is usually bought by weight, specify the number and size of specific items like onions, carrots or potatoes, use liquid measures for liquids and spoon measures for small amounts. It may look odd but the recipe will be easier to prepare.

As far as possible in this book I have used descriptive terms like teaspoons, dessertspoons, tablespoons, handfuls, and I have used them consistently. A spoonful (tea, dessert or table) means a rounded spoonful except for liquids. A pinch is the amount you can pick up between your thumb and forefinger (less than one eighth of a teaspoon.) A handful of chopped parsley means the amount of parsley you can pick up from the chopping board without using your other hand to stuff it in. A clove of garlic means a clove the size of one of the big outer cloves from the Spanish, Italian or Israeli garlic bulbs commonly available in your supermarket. If the inner cloves are thinner and smaller than the outer cloves then use two or three of them. If I say a small clove of garlic I mean one of these inner cloves or half a big one.

Cups, Pints, Millilitres and Liquid Ounces

The commonest problem in working with recipes is the confusion caused by the fact that there is a difference between the standard American cup-measure and the "cup" measure used in Ireland and Gt. Britain.

There is also a problem caused by the fact that some tins and jars are marked on their labels in millilitres and some in fluid ounces. I have standardised on the most commonly available heatproof glass measuring jug which measures 500 millilitres or 20 fluid ounces (1 pint) and has a millilitre and a fluid ounce scale marked on its side.

For smaller amounts of dry ingredients like flour or rice I will use spoon measures and for larger quantities I will always use fluid ounces. A recipe which calls for 4 fluid ounces of rice means dry, uncooked rice poured into this measuring jug up to the mark measuring 4 fluid ounces. This is much the simplest method.

Where it is usual to buy an ingredient like meat or fish by weight then the recipes will call for so many ounces of mince or fresh cod.

If you should use recipes from other books you should check at the beginning of the book to see what the author says about weights and measures. In most cases, if you stick firmly to one system for all the measures you should not have problems.

The table below is laid out for you to be able to look up the equivalent amounts in the metric and imperial systems and lays out the scale of graded oven temperature descriptions in common use with the equivalent temperature in degrees centigrade, degrees Fahrenheit and Gas Marks.

OVEN TEMPERATURES

Description	°Fahrenheit	°Centigrade	Gas Mark
Cool	225	110	$\frac{1}{4}$
	250	120	$\frac{1}{2}$
Very	275	140	1
Moderate	300	150	2
	320	160	3
Moderate	350	180	4
Medium	375	190	5
Hot	400	200	6
	425	220	7
Very Hot	450	230	8
	475	240	9
Extremely Hot	500	260	10

LIQUID MEASURES

Imperial	Metric
1/4 pint (5 fl. oz)	142 millilitres
1/2 pint (10 fl. oz)	284 mls
1 pint (20 fl. oz)	568 mls
1 quart (2 pints)	1.136 litres
4 quarts (1 gallon)	4.54 litres

WEIGHTS

Imperial	Metric	Metric Recipe
1 ounce (oz)	28.34 grammes	30 g
4 ozs ($\frac{1}{4}$ lb)	113.36 g	100 g
8 ozs ($\frac{1}{2}$ lb)	225.00 g	250 g
16 ozs (1 lb)	453.44 g	450 g
	500.00 g	$\frac{1}{2}$ Kilo
32 ozs (2 lbs)	906.88 g	900 g
35 ozs (2 lbs 3oz)	991.90 g	1000 g (1 Kilo)

Nutrition and Your Health

Nutrition is one of those subjects which, when it turns up, as it does with increasing frequency, as a topic on the radio or television, makes otherwise balanced people dive for cover. There are times when I think that some "nutritionists" have become a health hazard themselves. You must remember that many "nutritionists" are not nutritional experts at all; some are journalists who specialise in the area of consumer affairs; many are consultants retained by different sectors of the food manufacturing industry to promote their products or denigrate those of their rivals; others are just cranks with their own particular dietary axe to grind. Some "nutritionists" have given nutrition a bad name, creating an image of the subject in the mind of the public that it is boring, complicated and aimed at preventing us from eating our favourite foods.

But nutrition is not about giving up particular foods at all. Nutrition is about eating enough of the right foods. There is broad agreement among real health and nutritional experts about what constitutes a balanced diet. A balanced diet is one which provides sufficient energy and adequate amounts of the different proteins, vitamins, minerals and dietary fibre which the human body needs to maintain good health and vitality.

There is general agreement that the "typical" diet eaten by the "average" person in advanced "western" countries is not balanced. This mythical person eats too much fat (particularly "saturated" fat), too much salt, too much sugar and too little dietary fibre. But this certainly does not mean that if you eat a bowl of bran for breakfast, cut the fat off any meat you eat, refrain from sprinkling salt on your dinner, and don't put sugar in your coffee that you will be eating a balanced diet. All of these actions would contribute towards improved health but in

13

themselves they are not sufficient to combat the effects of a badly planned diet. Unless they are backed up by a properly balanced diet these dietary improvements cannot by themselves prevent the development of high blood pressure, higher than average cholesterol levels, or constipation.

No single food can be said to be "bad" for you. (With the obvious exception of foods which exacerbate an existing, diagnosed medical problem in a specific individual.) Foods only become bad for you within the context of all the other things you eat, the amount of energy you expend, your medical health. It is equally true that you cannot survive by eating just one food. It really is a question of balance.

The stereotypical image many people have of Italians is that they are fat from eating too much pasta and olive oil. In fact, most Italians are not fat at all and they have just about the lowest incidence of food-related heart disease in Europe. The average Italian certainly does consume lots of pasta and olive oil but does so in a context of hard work for extremely long hours, and in a diet which includes far more fish, far more good bread, far more fresh fruits and vegetables, far more raw salads, much less meat, much less processed food and far fewer "sweets" than would be normal in this country.

So what should you eat? To eat a balanced diet you need to eat some foods in relatively greater quantities than others. If you imagine the total amount of food you eat in any one day as a dinner plate then the different types of food in your diet for each day should break down in roughly the proportions shown. (See Diagram)

A BALANCED DIET
FOOD TYPES

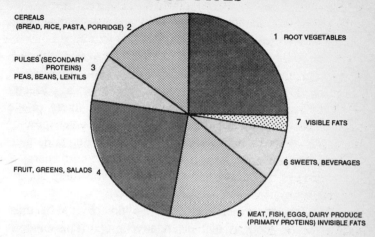

No one is saying that this must be followed precisely. But if the rough proportions of the different types of foods in your diet do not nearly correspond with the proportions shown in the diagram then you are not balancing your daily intake of food. You might think that you could look at the picture over a full week and that might make it easier to achieve the balance. It doesn't really work that way.

For instance, almost three-quarters of the diagram is taken up by root vegetables, cereal products (mainly wholemeal bread, rice, pasta, and breakfast cereals like porridge or muesli), plant proteins from pulses (peas, beans of all types, lentils), and fresh fruit, green vegetables and salads. All of these foods contain relatively high proportions of dietary fibre. If you do not eat the correct proportion of these foods each day, but binge on fruit and vegetables once a week, your body could be lacking sufficient fibre for six days of the week.

Look at it another way. Something less than a third of the balanced daily diet is taken up by meat, fish, eggs, nuts, dairy produce (cheese, yoghurt, milk), visible fats (butter, margarine, oils, and the fat on meat), sweets, and drinks other than water. It is actually easier to balance your diet if you make every meal of the day conform roughly to the proportions shown. This means that a breakfast of an orange, one grilled rasher with two slices of wholemeal bread, a grilled tomato and a cup of tea or coffee is much closer to the ideal balance than two rashers, a sausage, a fried egg, a slice of fried white bread and four cups of sweet tea. You would probably feel better after it as well.

On the other hand, a small bowl of a good muesli (one without added sugar or sweetener) might be a perfectly balanced breakfast but insufficient for you in terms of the energy content you need to start the day. It's never quite as simple as it looks because every body is different (small-framed, medium build, large framed) and people burn energy at different rates depending upon the type of work they do, the amount of physical exercise they take, even the time of the day (or night) they are at their most energetic and active. What most experts agree about is that the relative proportions of each different type of food should be more or less as shown in the diagram.

If an individual gets roughly 3 to 4 ounces of meat, fish, or dairy protein, or rather more than this of plant proteins (pulses), each day then, as long as they are getting sufficient quantities in proportion of all the other food types, their diet will be in balance. If they are constantly burning off more than usual amounts of energy through increased sporting activity or hard physical work then they should stoke up by increasing the amount of carbohydrates they consume. The carbohydrates are all found in that section of the diagram covered by cereals, pulses, fruit, green vegetables and root vegetables.

None of this is particularly revolutionary. It comes very close to the traditional breakdown of a good Sunday lunch into "meat or fish, potatoes and two veg." The mistake a great many people make is that they take large portions of meat and very little of the potatoes and two vegetables. It should be the other way round. "Potatoes and two veg with a little meat or fish."

This theory is relatively straightforward if you confine yourself to eating real food and by that I mean food which has not been through a manufacturing process or had "value" added to it by a food manufacturer. Today people tend to eat much more processed food. Our "excessive" consumption of fat, sugar and salt tends to be hidden in these foods rather than easily visible on our plates.

The difficulty faced by food manufacturers is that fat, sugar, salt, together with a vast array of stabilisers, emulsifiers, colourings and flavour enhancers, are needed either to give longer shelf-life to their products, to restore some of the attractiveness the food loses during the manufacturing process, or simply to disguise the fact that some products are made from less than "prime cut" ingredients. These additives are not easily replaced.

I am not saying that you should not eat these foods but that you should be aware that many of them contain disproportionately high amounts of hidden fats, salts and sugars. If you habitually derive much of your nourishment from processed foods then it can be difficult to know exactly what you are eating. This makes it all the more difficult to plan a balanced, healthy diet.

The table below shows into which category in the diagram most commonly available foodstuffs fall.

FOOD CATEGORIES

CEREALS

Grains of all kinds and the products made from them. Wheat (breads, pasta), oats (porridge), rice, maize (corn flakes, popcorn), bulghur, couscous, noodles, muesli, biscuits.

PLANT PROTEINS (PULSES)

All types of beans and peas both fresh (french beans, mange-tout, runner, bean sprouts) and dried (lentils, kidney beans, haricot beans, chickpeas, mung, lima and tinned baked beans).

ROOT VEGETABLES

Potatoes, carrots, turnips, parsnips, onions, garlic, leeks, beetroot, celeriac, artichokes, yams, sweet potatoes, fennel.

FRUITS, GREENS and SALADS

Apples, oranges, grapefruits, lemons, grapes, melon, plums, strawberries, raspberries, blackcurrants, kiwi, pears, etc. Cabbage, broccoli, brussels sprouts, spinach, parsley. All fresh herbs, lettuce, tomatoes, olives, cucumber, mushrooms, courgettes, aubergines, scallions, radishes, watercress.

HIGH PROTEIN FOODS

Meats, fish, poultry, eggs, nuts, milk, cheese, yoghurt.

SWEETS and BEVERAGES

Confectionery, puddings, milk-shakes, dried and candied fruits, chocolate, jam, marmalade, tinned fruits, alcohol, fruit-juice, tea, coffee, lemonades and soft drinks, lollipops, ice-cream.

VISIBLE FATS

Butter, margarine, vegetable and dairy spreads, oils, lard, dripping, bacon fat, meat fat, pies, sausages, croissants, sausage rolls, pastries, steak and kidney pudding, suet crust.

Breakfast like a king
Lunch like a Lord
Dine like a pauper.

That old adage may make nutritional sense but is it practicable when you have to plan, shop, and cook for yourself as well as do a full day's work or study? Well, I would suggest that it is probably correct in aim.

You should attempt to get up in time to eat a good breakfast. You have, after all, been fasting all night and the body works more efficiently if it gets balanced fuel regularly rather than in large unbalanced dollops. Furthermore, I would suggest that your body does not need to be heavily fuelled late in the evening just before it goes to sleep for several hours. And yet people refuse to adjust their eating habits to fit in with this perfectly obvious fact.

A good breakfast does not have to be the traditional cooked breakfast but it should be sustaining enough to see you through until lunch-time. Suggestions for easy to prepare, fast-to-eat breakfasts are included in the recipe section.

If you eat lunch in a canteen, cafe, or pub, then it is more than likely that it will be a meal composed, in the main, of processed foods. It may fill a gap, fuel you up to a greater or lesser extent, but it is unlikely to be balanced in nutritional terms.

So, at worst, we are left with the fact that you must make it your business to make and eat at least one meal a day which is balanced or attempts to correct the balance of all the rest of the food you have eaten during the day. In practice I think that you might have to settle for eating one balanced meal a day which you prepare yourself.

This meal should contain a portion of food which is rich in protein. This can be meat, fish, poultry, eggs, nuts, cheese or pulses like beans or lentils. You should vary the type of protein in each meal and the recipe section has been planned in a way which allows you to do this. There are some essential fatty acids which the body needs and which it cannot manufacture for itself from other foods. This is why you should include a "fatty"

19

fish (trout, salmon, herring, mackerel, sardines, pilchards) and liver in your diet at least once a week and consume moderate amounts of oil, margarine or butter.

Your meal should contain carbohydrates in the form of a cereal food, or good wholemeal bread, rice, pasta, or root vegetables and tubers like potatoes. It should also have generous amounts, in proportion to the protein content, of fresh vegetables and fresh fruit or salads. These are an essential source of vitamins, minerals and trace elements not found in other foods. Vary the types you eat and eat them raw whenever possible.

Another consequence of eating large amounts of processed foods is that your diet can become seriously deficient in the amount of dietary fibre needed for your intestinal tract to function efficiently. The closer a food is to its natural state when eaten, the higher the fibre content is likely to be. One of those modern marketing "myths" is that wheat bran breakfast cereals are the only readily available source of dietary fibre. This is not true. They are one source but they can contain large amounts of unnecessary sugar. The outer husk of all grains is a good source of fibre, but the body needs a balanced mixture of cereal fibre and the fibre from fruit and vegetables. If you eat a properly balanced diet containing lots of root vegetables, fresh fruits and salads, wholemeal breakfast cereals and bread, you should not need "extra" fibre in the form of bran. An excess of bran can prevent the absorption of iron from food, if not actually leach it out of your system.

Fats, Oils and Visible Fats

Fat in your diet divides up into three main types:

    a) Saturated fats
    b) Poly-unsaturated fats and oils
    c) Mono-unsaturated fats and oils

Fats in the diet are a complicated subject. Fats make food palatable and your body needs to take in fat because it is energy rich — a very small amount provides a lot of energy. You are not trying to eat a fat-less diet but trying to control the amount of energy you take in the form of fat and to change the balance of the types of fat that you eat.

At the moment, the "average" person receives about 40% of his energy requirement in the form of fat. Most experts agree that this should be reduced. They disagree about the size of the reduction required; some say 5%, others 10%. They all agree that the proportion of saturated fat in the diet should be reduced substantially in relation to the other types. The reason why most dieticians advocate the reduction of what they call "visible fats" is because they know that we are eating large quantities of hidden fats in other foods, particularly processed foods.

Saturated fat is suited to the food manufacturing process because it does not go rancid as quickly as the other types and so adds to the shelf life of processed foods. Cakes, biscuits, pies, sausages of all kinds, pâté, croissants, pastries, suet puddings, cheese, nuts, meat and fish all contain substantial amounts of hidden fat of all types.

Visible fats are those fats and oils which we can actually see.

Fats which are high in saturated fat are butter, lard, suet, and the fat, both visible and hidden, in meat and meat products and in most processed baked foods.

Fats which are high in poly-unsaturated fats are vegetable oils like sunflower oil, and corn oil.

The most outstanding example of an oil very rich in mono-unsaturated fatty acids is olive oil.

The recommendations for adjusting the ratio of saturated to unsaturated fats in your diet are pretty straightforward. You should cut down on fatty meats, processed foods like sausages pies and pastries, salamis. (There is a lot of saturated fat in most pâtés but, because they are made from liver, on balance I would not recommend reducing your consumption of them.) Use a spread based on a poly-unsaturated vegetable oil instead of butter on your bread. Where you must cook a food in fat then use a vegetable oil or a good olive oil which should also be used for salad dressings.

Sugar in Your Diet

Sugar has no nutrients. It is converted into pure energy. The "average" person consumes about 100 lbs. of sugar each year, most of this in a "hidden" form in sweets, soft drinks, alcohol, biscuits, cakes, breakfast cereals, tinned fruits, fruit juices and, believe it or not, in savoury processed foods. Eating foods which are high in sugar reduces your appetite for more nutritious foods and rots your teeth. If you are eating a well-balanced diet which provides you with all your energy needs there is absolutely no justification for eating sugar at all. You get any sugars your body needs from natural sugars in fruit and vegetables.

Salt in your Diet

The main use of salt in foods was as a preservative. Processed foods contain high amounts of salt for this very reason. Salt is no more than a bad habit from the days when it was difficult to preserve foods, particularly meats, without it. Never add salt to your food without first tasting it and add salt in very small amounts at the cooking stage, never at the table. Avoid crisps, salted nuts and packet soups which contain very high levels of salt.

How to Shop

One of the generally un-sung pleasures of cooking for yourself is that you can eat what you like, whenever you feel like doing so. It has always been a mystery to me that, despite the vast range of foodstuffs available today, most families eat a very restricted diet. One reason for this, probably the main one, is that the regular range of dishes prepared in a family is a usually a compromise between the likes and dislikes of various members of the household.

I know one family where one son will not eat any meat except pork fillet; his brother refuses any dish that has onions in it; and the family head refuses to accept that he has eaten a meal at all unless it contains a great slab of meat, preferably grilled sirloin steak! The result is that the poor cook in the household breaks her back and racks her brains every day trying to come up with three separate meals. Most of us have the common sense not to indulge that particular form of insanity but the result can be a restricted range of dishes that everyone will eat.

One of the joys of being on your own is that you can eat all your own favourites but you can also experiment and expand your tastes. I promise you that you will discover a whole new world of food.

Planning Meals
There are two schools of thought on this subject. The first says that if you sit down and plan your meals for a whole week ahead and from this draw up a shopping list, you will, with care, eat a balanced and varied diet and not overspend; the second maintains that such planning creates a rigid shopping list and a blinkered mind which prevents you from taking full advantage of special offers and so robs you of the joy of trying out some

new food which catches your fancy.

For instance you may have decided on whiting but the fishmonger has a glut of mackerel and is selling at a giveaway price; the butcher has had a run on expensive cuts of spring lamb and is desperately trying to shift his surplus breast of lamb at suicidal rates. The answer, obvious as it may seem, is to make your plans, draw up your list, but be prepared to modify it when you see real bargains.

Shopping

Cooking for one person is usually regarded as being more expensive than catering for two. This is true up to a point but careful planning can cut down on waste and reduce the difference in cost substantially. What each person can afford to spend on food each week will vary but you must sit down and work out some sort of realistic budget which will allow you to spend enough for a reasonable breakfast and a balanced evening meal every day. Almost all of the meals in this book can be prepared for no more than it will cost you for a "hamburger meal out" and will be a jolly sight better for you.

Do investigate the shops in your area further than the nearest "twenty-four-hour-shop-on-the-corner". That may be convenient but it will always be far more expensive than a market-stall or even a supermarket. The range of fresh foodstuffs available in corner shops is usually very limited (and often less than fresh) and convenience foods, while undeniably convenient, cost more and are less nutritious. Specialist shops like butchers, fishmongers, bakers and vegetable shops are normally cheaper for fresh foods than supermarkets. Supermarkets offer best value in general groceries, packeted and tinned foods, cereals and household goods.

In an ideal world you would shop in a high street where there are all sorts of shops and that will at least cut down drastically on the time you spend shopping.

Buy the quantities you want

Just because a supermarket sells lemons in bags of ten or bread rolls in a packet of eight does not mean you have to buy them that way. My local supermarket has a prominent sign saying that they will halve a pack of anything! I have never put them to the test on a packet of corn flakes or a bag of rice but I have with fresh foods and they do it cheerfully. If your local supermarket will not oblige take your custom to one that will. But do give them a chance by asking the manager first.

The Butcher, The Baker, The Candlestick-maker

Make friends with your butcher, and the baker, the man or woman in the vegetable shop and the fishmonger's.

Many people are shy of going into a specialist shop like a butcher's because they are unsure of what to ask for or how much it might cost. While it is true that many specialist shops do not do enough to encourage "learner-cooks," (their labelling and pricing policies can be as much of a mystery to their staff as to the customer), it is equally true that many of them are delighted to be asked for advice and are always willing to help. One of the oldest tricks in the shopping veteran's handbook is to avoid the young, good-looking apprentice and ask the mature, balding butcher or the motherly-looking fishmonger for advice.

Frantic Friday evenings and rushed Saturdays when the shops have queues out into the street are not the times to shop if you need help and advice. Choose a quiet time. If you get into a pattern of shopping mid-week you will find that specialist shopkeepers have another side to their characters. They are proud of their knowledge and the skills of their trades and most of them are happy to help you with the benefit of their experience.

Butchers

Many butchers have free charts and leaflets supplied by their trade organisations and meat marketing people and can often get you a copy. This is probably the simplest way of getting to recognise the main cuts of meat and their uses. Display it in your kitchen and refer to it when planning your meals for the week.

Look out for a butcher who labels his meat clearly with the correct names. Avoid those who sell meat labelled "for stewing" or "for frying." There should always be a clear and well-displayed current price-list so that you can work out what you can afford and what is good value. Butchers tend to display the cheaper cuts of meat early in the week and some will only have things like liver and lamb hearts or tripes on certain days. Liver is a good test of a butcher. Those who have it every day might be buying it in bulk, deep-frozen, whereas the butcher who only has liver, say, on Thursdays, is probably preparing it himself from his own carcases and it is more likely to be fresh. Most butchers concentrate on joints and prime-cuts at the end of the week, which is when the demand for them is greatest. A butcher who will happily trim and bone meat for you on a weekday may turn into a snarling monster if you ask him to do the same on a busy Saturday morning.

Fishmongers
Fishmongers, alas, are a dying breed, killed off by our passion for frozen fish-fingers. If there is a good wet-fish shop in your area then use it. It will usually have a greater range of fish than all but the biggest supermarket and the fish will be fresher, cheaper and be stored and displayed in better conditions. Look out in your area for a large covered-market and pay it a visit, as fishmongers tend to lurk in corners of these markets where they have had a stall or a shop for generations. Don't shop for fish on Mondays or immediately after bank holiday weekends. Fishmongers, too, will be happy to advise you and will usually fillet, bone, or sell you the exact amount that you need. Most fishes are interchangeable when it comes to recipes so don't be afraid to try unusual fish.

Bakers
A tricky one this. When my son was small he used to distinguish between "real" bread and "imaginary" bread. It's a good distinction. Real bread is baked and sold by real bakers, usually in small shops with the bakery attached to them, or baked by you at home. Real bread has a rich satisfying texture and taste and is an excellent and nutritious food. It also has the most wonderful aroma known to man when it is being baked.

Unfortunately for you, imaginary bread also has a wonderful aroma when it is baking. There the resemblance ends. "Hot Bread Shops," which live at the entrance to many large supermarkets and in many high streets, rely upon this smell to sell their imaginary breads which taste just as spongy, rubbery and bland as any factory sliced pan (whether white or dyed brown) even though they come in a myriad shapes and under countless "country-kitchen" names.

If you like imaginary bread, fine, eat it but buy small loaves so that you do not have to struggle through a large sliced pan for a week or, worse still, throw it away and buy another half-way through. I promise you that once you find a real baker you will never want to eat imaginary bread again. Yes, it does cost slightly more, but you can buy it in much smaller sizes and there is rarely any waste.

One tip. Check out small, local ethnic food shops for real breads. I happen to have a Jewish shop nearby which bakes the most wonderful, mouth-watering breads which are only on sale in that one shop.

Fruit and Vegetables

All other things being equal, an apple or an orange bought in a corner shop late at night will cost about twice as much as the same fruit bought from a supermarket or specialist fruit shop. Fruit and vegetables should be as fresh as possible and a good specialist retailer will buy his goods more frequently, in quantities which match his customers' demands rather than gluts in the market. Supermarkets in particular have a habit of selling off surpluses of fruit which has passed its sell-by date, pre-packed, in cellophane bags at knock-down prices.

Fruit and vegetables, contrary to popular belief, need very careful storage and display conditions. But the display conditions in large supermarkets, warm brightly-lit cabinets with the goods piled up in mounds, are the very conditions under which fruits and vegetables deteriorate quickest and lose their vitamin content. Fruit and vegetables need cool, dark conditions. The reason continental shops display their fruit and vegetables in the open air is that their customers buy fruit and vegetables regularly in small quantities, often shopping for them every day.

I know this may not always be practical for you but try to shop for vegetables at least twice a week rather than buying them all at once. Eat leafy green vegetables as soon as possible after you buy them. Root vegetables will keep rather longer.

The Emergency Store Cupboard

To the most organised person on earth will come a day on which they forget to shop, get hi-jacked by friends on the way to the shops, or just run out of money. You will arrive home tired, hungry, penniless and miserable. This is what the emergency store cupboard is all about.

The theory behind it is that each week, or whenever you shop, you buy one item, maybe two or three if you happen to be flush that week, which are laid down against such emergencies. Obviously these must be things which will keep for long periods. This is where tins come into their own. Always check the "use-by" dates on items in your cupboard and rotate the cans and packs in your store when you add to it. It is very easy for an item to get pushed to the back and forgotten until long after the date by which it should have been used.

The list which follows is only a guide. I'm not suggesting for a moment that you must have all of these. But if you build up an emergency store along these lines you need never fear the occasional period when funds are really tight or when shopping becomes a real hassle.

Cereal Products

 1 packet of your favourite pasta
 1 packet of long-grain rice
 1 packet of porridge oats
 1 packet of strong white plain flour
 1 small tin of baking powder
 1 small tin of dried active yeast

Dairy Products

    1 tin of dried milk
    1 packet of vacuum-packed mature cheddar cheese

Tinned Protein

    1 tin sardines or skippers (brisling) in oil or tomato sauce
    1 small tin tuna fish
    1 tin of baby clams
    1 tin of anchovy fillets in olive oil.

Vegetables and Pulses

    1-2 tins or jars of Italian plum tomatoes (chopped)
    1 jar of a good quality pasta sauce (Ragu brand is very good)
    1 tin red kidney beans
    1 tin haricot beans or Egyptian brown beans (Ful Medames)
    1 tin houmous (pureed chickpeas)
    1 packet of instant dried potatoes
    1 packet of dried lentils

Fresh Foods

You should never run out of the following fresh foods.

    Onions
    garlic
    eggs
    potatoes
    lettuce
    vacuum pack of rashers
    bottle of good quality olive oil
    bottle of lemon juice
    bottle of wine vinegar
    jar of good quality mayonnaise (Hellmann's)

Herbs and Spices

You should always have at least the following basics.

Whole black peppercorns

dried thyme, marjoram or oregano

Some very useful extras are:

whole cumin seeds

whole coriander seeds

ground turmeric

Sharwood's garam masala

ground paprika

small jar of creamed horseradish sauce (Burgess's is good)

You should try to buy a jar of a particular spice each week until you build up your collection. With the exception of turmeric, paprika and garam masala (which is a mixture of different spices) you should buy whole spices and grind them as you need them with your mortar and pestle. As long as you keep the jars tightly shut away from sunlight they keep well.

For the Fridge

If you have a fridge then you might consider the following list.

a small vacuum pack of smoked mackerel

a small vacuum pack of your favourite salami sausage

a packet of frozen pitta bread

a small carton of fresh cream

some fresh tomatoes

a green or red pepper

spring onions (scallions)

whole black olives in brine

Recipes

You will find that a number of the recipes in this book are based upon items from your emergency food store. This is quite deliberate. There's no use having such a store if you do not know how to make use of it and using some of the items from your store regularly will allow you to keep it up-to-date and prevent the less durable items going to waste.

Food Hygiene and You

Safe Shopping and Housekeeping

Good hygiene is essential at all stages of the food chain. Hygiene is defined as those conditions and practices in the storage, handling and preparation of food which are conducive to health. Consumer hygiene begins with careful shopping.

Most food growers and manufacturers go to a great deal of trouble and expense to ensure that their products leave their factories in a safe condition. They are the first link in the food hygiene chain. Remember that we are not talking here about the quality of their products but about their safety.

The next link in the chain is the retail outlet. No one but a criminal sets out to sell unsafe or contaminated food to the public but careless practices can quickly turn safe food into contaminated food. The most stringent storage and handling procedures are essential even in the cleanest environment.

The third link in the food hygiene chain is the home. There is absolutely no point in demanding that food manufacturers and retailers have higher standards of hygiene than you are prepared to practise at home. You are just as likely to contaminate food at home if you do not treat it correctly as any retailer.

Any shop which sells food should be clean and well-maintained. The guidelines are straight-forward and simple.

- All equipment, fittings, floors, counters, walls and windows should be spotless and well-maintained.

- All staff should be clean: clothes, hands, fingernails, hair. They should not have sores or skin infections, particularly on their hands, and cuts should never be uncovered but enclosed in a protective dressing.

- No animals should be permitted to enter the premises even when carried by their owners.

- Smoking should not be permitted.

- Foodstuffs in the shop and in any storage areas should never be exposed to direct sunlight, dirt, flies or, needless to say, vermin or animals of any kind.

- Perishable foods, dairy produce, meats (raw and cooked), fish (raw and cooked), cream or cheese cakes should be stored in refrigerated cabinets. These cabinets must be clean, working properly, rust free, and packed only to the storage line or the manufacturer's recommended level.

- Raw and cooked foods (particularly meats, poultry, and fish) must never be displayed together, served from the same part of the counter, served with the same utensils, or handled directly by the same staff, unless they use a new disposable cellophane plastic glove for each separate item.

While it will rarely be possible for you to check each and every one of these items, you may be sure that any establishment which breaks any of the more obvious, visible rules is unlikely to abide by those which are hidden from the public.

Shop Carefully
As well as taking your custom only to shops which show clear evidence of taking care in the storage, preparation and serving of their produce you should shop extremely carefully even in those that do.

- Never buy dairy produce, cooked or vacuum-packed foods except from a refrigerated storage cabinet or display counter.

- Always check the date stamp or sell-by date.

- Never buy food in a vacuum-pack (even from a refrigerated cabinet) if it is " blown" or the pack looks as if it has air in it.

- Tins should be free from dents, bulging at the ends, rust, or any kind of marks at the joints which might conceivably be caused by seepage.

- Use your sense of smell—meat should not smell "high" or fish "strong."

- Fresh fruit and vegetables should not be bruised, discoloured or have yellowed leaves.

- If fruit or vegetables are sold pre-packed always check for damaged or rotten items, or for any signs of wetness or sliminess in the pack. Ask for any that are wet or damaged to be removed and replaced and for the packing to be changed because they will already have contaminated the other items in the bag.

Food Poisoning

You can poison yourself by eating food which is naturally poisonous (which no one in their right mind does deliberately), or by eating food which has been contaminated by bacteria, toxic substances caused by bacterial action, or chemicals. Most bacteria are harmless (some actually beneficial) but a small percentage of them can poison. Some, like Clostridium botulinum, can create an extremely poisonous protein (botulin) which causes acute, often fatal, food-poisoning. Others are slightly less dangerous, but, particularly in small children or adults weakened by illness or old-age, can have results no less severe. Given the right conditions, of temperature and surroundings, a single-cell bacterium can multiply a million-fold in a few hours.

If you remember that food reaches us through many stages of growth, handling, preparation, storage, cooking—and if you think of each of these stages as a link in a continuous chain, then it is obvious that contamination can occur at any stage of the chain. Once a food has been contaminated it can contaminate other foods on contact with either the contaminated food itself or with surfaces, machines, implements or people who have been in contact with it. Hygiene is a system of practices and conditions designed to break this connective chain. Since I began to prepare this book the whole issue of salmonella in eggs has blown up and died down. You should be aware that there is a definite risk attached to the eating of eggs raw or partially-cooked eggs. I, in common with many other food writers, have gone on eating raw and lightly cooked eggs without the slightest problem. If you are nervous then do not prepare home-made mayonnaise and always cook your boiled, poached or fried eggs thoroughly.

Cool, Clean and Covered

The golden rules of hygiene are keep it cool, keep it clean and keep it covered.

While it is obviously common sense that foods bought from a refrigerated cabinet in a shop should be stored in a refrigerator when you get them home, meat, fish and most cooked foods should also be stored there as well. Fridges normally have an operating temperature between 3-5°C, which is cool enough to stop bacteria multiplying. You should check regularly to see that your fridge maintains this temperature range, defrosting it regularly and checking the door-seals.

Never put hot food, particularly soup (especially if it is in a hot bowl), into the fridge as this can cause a temporary rise in the internal temperature of the cabinet and can cause condensation on the walls which can produce favourable conditions for the growth of harmful bacteria.

Never allow juices to drip from one food onto another. Deep-frozen meat should be kept in a covered bowl while thawing because plastic freezer bags will not prevent it dripping. Food which is to be eaten without any further cooking should be stored on the top shelf of the fridge as a precaution against drips. Raw and cooked foods should never be allowed to come into contact in the fridge.

Perishable foods (vegetables, dairy produce, raw and cooked

meats, soups, stocks, baked pies, raw and cooked fish, eggs, vacuum packs, leftovers) should all be stored in a fridge. Food from opened tins should be decanted from the tin into a bowl and covered with cling film before storage.

Never leave food uncovered on the dining-table and store bread and biscuits in covered containers to avoid contamination from dust and flies.

Food Preparation

You cannot cook without handling food and this is the link in the hygiene chain where home practices are most likely to break down. Clean hands, utensils and work surfaces are essential.

Remember that food which is to receive no further cooking must never come into contact with raw food of any kind. Never use the same chopping board, work surface or utensil for both raw and cooked foods.

Good Hygiene Practices

- Wash your hands thoroughly and clean your fingernails before handling any food.

  Wash your hands thoroughly after using the lavatory or handling pets.

- Clean surfaces and utensils at each separate stage of the preparation of food.

- Use separate work surfaces for cooked and raw foods.

- Be particularly careful when preparing packed lunches or sandwiches as these may spend several hours at room temperature before they are eaten.

- Put food into the correct storage conditions as soon as possible after purchase.

- Always clean, dress and cover any cuts or sores with waterproof dressings before handling food.

- Try not to touch your face, hair or body while preparing food.

35

- Keep pets strictly away from food preparation areas.

- Always put food into drip-proof containers in the fridge.

- Use leftovers as soon as possible.

- Do not keep food "warm" for long periods.

- Reheated food and "cook-chill" products should be piping hot all the way through—follow the manufacturer's instructions correctly.

- Always follow standing-time instructions for microwave-cooked food.

- Wage war relentlessly on flies.

Delf and Cutlery, Dishcloths and Washing Up

The dishes from which you eat and the cutlery you use are the final link in the hygiene chain. Bacteria thrive best on moist, warm surfaces. Your dishes and cutlery need to be thoroughly washed in water which is at least 46°C (140°F) using a detergent. They should then be rinsed in really hot water of at least 77°F (195°F) and left to drain in an upright condition. This avoids contamination from damp, dirty dish-cloths.

Finally, invest in a bottle of Milton sterilising fluid. Yes, I do mean the stuff for baby's bottles! Regularly soak all your dish-cloths and plastic washing-up brushes and sponges in it overnight.

How to Cook

How to Cook

The title of this chapter, though ambitious in the extreme, is not really as silly as it sounds. By now you should have planned your meals for the week, bought the ingredients, and quite possibly be standing facing a cooker with a knife in one hand and this book in the other. Do not turn the knife on yourself — Yet!

You will find that many of the dishes in this book do not need "cooking" at all and that is quite deliberate. Let me offer you a word of advice before you start on any of those which do.

Very often what separates an experienced cook from a novice is the state of the kitchen afterwards. It is my belief that the thing which puts off a great many novice cooks is the amount of clearing-up and washing-up which they have to do after they've prepared and eaten their meal. Novices tend to be impulsive and go into the attack without planning, leaving a litter of pots, pans, dishes, and packets all over the kitchen. The forlorn cry of "It's just not worth it for myself!" is usually a symptom of post-prandial depression caused by the thought of having to clear up this mess.

Cooking should be a relaxed, pleasing experience and you should set out deliberately to make it so. If I am cooking for myself the first thing I do is bring the radio into the kitchen and find an interesting programme to listen to—words, not music, because you have to listen to the words. If I am following a recipe, and I frequently do, then I work out which parts of the meal will take the longest cooking time. I lay out the ingredients for that dish and the implements I will need in its preparation. Then, feeling virtuous, I pour myself a smidgeon of alcohol or make a cup of tea, depending on the hour of the day and my mood. Only then do I start "cooking," clearing up as I go, not letting it pile up. When the part of the meal which takes the longest amount of cooking time is underway I start on the next longest, usually the vegetables or the salad. I clear up again, then set the table or the tray or whatever.

There is a temptation, to which I've noticed my own son and the children of friends fall prey, to eat out of the pan, or standing up in the kitchen, on the dubious grounds that "it saves washing-up." It doesn't. I strongly recommend that you dish up onto a hot serving dish and then serve yourself from that at the table onto a hot dinner plate. There are three good reasons for doing this. First, you will appreciate your food more and reduce the risk of mouth-scalding and indigestion; second, you will be less likely to over-eat; third, you could, as a result of not over-eating, have some useful leftovers to use on another day.

COOKING METHODS

This section of the book is intended as a primer in the basic methods of cooking foods:

    Boiling
    Simmering
    Steaming
    Stewing, braising, casseroles,
    Grilling
    Frying : shallow, pan and stir frying
    Roasting and baking
    Steaming

Each cooking method is illustrated by a "master recipe" (sometimes more than one), which is designed to teach you the fundamental principles of that method so that when you come to cook a recipe from the recipe section of the book and meet one of these basic methods you will know exactly what it means and how to achieve the best results.

BOILING

When you "boil" food you immerse it completely in a liquid (usually water) which has been pre-heated to boiling temperature and leave it there for the required cooking time. The word comes from the Latin word (through French) to "bubble" and this is the characteristic action of the liquid when it boils. Water boils at 100°C (212°F). In fact this temperature is often not ideal for cooking foods; too high for the proteins of meat and fish and really too low to cook vegetables quickly enough to preserve all their colour and vitamins. It was probably chosen as a method in the days before thermometers as a way to judge that the water was really hot before putting in the food. Safer than sticking in your finger.

Liquids at boiling temperature seethe and send up fierce streams of bubbles. Naturally, when you first put in the food the temperature drops a little and the boiling action stops momentarily. If you have sufficient water in the pot it will come back to the boil very quickly.

A food which absolutely must be boiled is pasta.

Master Recipe — Pasta

Pasta, even small amounts, "must" be boiled in lots of water. Italian cooks would use 4 litres of water to boil 450 grams (1 lb) of pasta. This is to keep the pasta pieces separate while cooking. If you use too little water the starch from the pasta becomes glutinous and the pasta sticks together. To help keep the pasta separate some cooks would add a drop of olive oil (vegetable oil will do just as well) to the boiling water before putting in the pasta. The oil coats the pasta as it passes through the surface of the boiling water.

450 grams of pasta will happily serve 3-4 people depending upon whether it is being served as a starter or a main course. You will not be eating anything like that amount so you can use less water. For pasta as a main course about one-third of a

41

pound of dried pasta is a generous helping. As dried pasta tends to come in 500 gram packets, you will be safe enough measuring about one-third of such a packet. For this you will need 3 pints (2 litres) of boiling water, or as near to this as your pot will hold.

It is usual to salt the water when boiling pasta. This has the effect of slightly raising the boiling temperature and this is the reason that some recipes for pasta seem to demand a great deal of salt to be added to the water. (It doesn't really make the pasta taste salty as most of it is thrown away with the cooking water.) For your amount of water 1 level teaspoon will be quite enough. If you are determined to avoid salt at all costs it is not absolutely necessary.

Put all the pasta into the boiling water at once and use a wooden spoon to make sure that long strands of spaghetti (which will soften very quickly) get completely immersed as quickly as possible. Give the water a good rapid stir to get the pasta swirling round the pot (to prevent initial sticking to the bottom) and put the lid on to bring it back to the boil as quickly as possible. Do not go away! It takes only seconds. Remove the lid and set it aside. Give the pasta another good stir and leave it to cook until it is done.

Pasta should only be cooked until it is what the Italians call "al dente," which means firm to the bite. Part of the joy of pasta is its texture and if you overcook it, until it is soft and mushy, you have lost most of the pleasure. How do you know when it is ready?

The cooking instructions on most packets suggest far too long a cooking-time. Although, I have come across a few, just to be confusing, which suggest too short a time. Pasta made in Italy tends to do this because the Italians like their pasta "molto al dente." You have to test it. Frequently. I have, in my time, heard some really weird testing methods, like taking a strand and throwing it against the wall. If it sticks it is cooked. If it is sticky enough to do that then it is cooked—to death!

You will have to experiment but as a starting point you should subtract three minutes from the cooking times suggested on pasta manufactured in this country and perhaps add one minute to the times suggested on Italian packets. Take a fork and extract one piece of pasta from the pot. Blow on it to cool it, then bite into it. It should be tender, with a little firmness, a little "bite" to it.

Drain it at once into a large strainer, shaking it to drain away all the water. Have ready a heated serving dish with a tablespoon of warm olive oil in the bottom. Tip in the pasta and using two forks mix the oil through it. If the recipe calls for grated cheese you should add half of it now and mix it through with the forks. Add the prepared sauce and mix it through. Now serve it immediately. You must not attempt to keep pasta warm. Your sauce and cheese should always be ready for the pasta not the other way round.

If you have trouble keeping the pasta from sticking together there are 4 possible causes. 1) It is overcooked. 2) The sauce was not added to it soon enough. 3) You have not served it quickly enough. 4) The pasta was stale before you cooked it. (Buy it in a supermarket where the turnover is large enough to prevent this happening.)

Although all pasta is made from the same basic dough there are literally dozens of different shapes and sizes. In my experience, the twisted shapes that look like thick corkscrews need a little more cooking than the packet suggests and so do the larger, slightly thicker macaroni (narrow hollow tube) types. But there is no substitute for testing.

The different shapes should also be considered in relation to the type of sauce that you are going to serve with the pasta. Some shapes work better with some sauces than with others. Meat sauces, for instance, work best with short macaroni or shell shapes because the sauce gets trapped in the hollows. Spaghetti is best with a straight, thick, tomato-based sauce. The delicate butterfly and twist shapes go best with light creamy sauces, or with very special sauces like pesto, or just warm olive oil and fresh herbs (basil or marjoram).

So-called "fresh" pasta which can sometimes be found in specialist shops and in some large supermarkets needs very little cooking—as little as 2-3 minutes for most types—because it has not been dried.

Master Recipe — Boiled Potatoes

Boiling vegetables is probably the least imaginative way of cooking them. However, you will meet recipes which call for you to part or "par" boil vegetables and there is a strong case to be argued for this being the best way to treat potatoes.

For one person you will need about 8 ozs. ($\frac{1}{2}$ lb.) of potato. This will usually work out at one large potato, two medium sized potatoes or four small ones.

One of the greatest problems with potatoes today is to manage to get good ones. Gone are the days, I'm afraid, when you could buy many different varieties. Today you are more likely to be faced with a quick choice between two—home-grown and foreign. I'm tempted to say that you'll recognise them at once by the simple fact that the foreign ones are "clean," in other words you don't have to buy a half-pound of mud to every two pounds of potatoes as you do with the home-grown variety.

Wash and scrub your potatoes well in cold water. I find that the plastic dish-washing brushes are the best implement for this. Cut away any bits that are scabby or discoloured. Throw away any green ones. If you intend to eat the potatoes plain-boiled then always boil them in their jackets. Bring water to the boil in a pot then put in the potatoes. The water should just cover them and the pot, ideally, should be just big enough to fit the potatoes without them swimming around in lots of water. Bring the water back to the boil then reduce the heat and put a lid on the pot. Cook them until they are tender. Try not to poke them too often to see if they are done. Only you will know when they are cooked to your liking. Most people like potatoes tender all the way through. Some prefer them "al dente" in the middle. This is the subject of many raging battles in my house and whoever cooks, wins.

Drain off the water completely and then return the potatoes to the pot. Cover them with a clean tea-towel and turn the heat down to very low, barely on, and let them dry out a little. They will keep this way without coming to any harm for several minutes while you serve up the rest of the meal.

This is the moment to skin them if you want to mash them or make a potato salad. Hold the potato in a cloth and, using a small sharp knife, peel back the skins. Most of the nutrients in potatoes are held just under the skin so peel away as little of the flesh as you can.

SIMMERING

This is another method of cooking by immersion in a hot liquid. In the case of simmering, however, the liquid is heated to just below its boiling point. You may have to bring the liquid to the boil and then turn down the heat to make sure that you have just the right temperature. When a liquid simmers its surface trembles rather than the strong bubbling you see when it boils. There are two rates of simmer. Recipes will usually say "simmer" or "simmer gently." To "simmer" implies a temperature of 96-98°C (205-209°F). A "gentle simmer" means a temperature of 82-87°C (180-189°F) and the water surface barely moves at this temperature.

The higher of these two heats works well for rice and beans, although some beans, like red kidney beans, must be boiled hard for ten minutes before reducing the heat in order to destroy harmful enzymes which can cause stomach upsets. Root vegetables are usually simmered. Gentle simmering is best for meats and for fish.

A stew should always be simmered (even if it is cooked in the oven), never boiled. A soup is often said to have been "spoiled" if it has been boiled and milk, or sauces containing milk, will "boil over" if they are "boiled."

Master Recipe — Dried Beans (Pulses)

This basic method applies to any dried pulse vegetable. All dried pulses except lentils need to be soaked before cooking and the time needed varies from bean to bean. Most pulses benefit from a minimum of three to four hours. So if you are going to cook them in the evening, then put them to soak in the morning. Some, like chickpeas, need to be soaked overnight. Never soak them for longer than twelve to fourteen hours otherwise fermentation can set in. With lentils you need to spread them out on a dry surface and check for tiny little pebbles and stones which you should pick out and throw away. Always wash beans in several changes of cold running water—they can be dirty and very dusty.

Cooking times for dried beans vary enormously as it depends upon the freshness of the dried bean. Very old ones require much longer cooking. You should buy your beans from a shop which specialises in them or from a supermarket whose turnover is high. Beans in little corner shops might lie on the shelf for many months before someone buys them.

The cooking times in the table below assume that the beans have already been soaked for the length of time suggested in the recipe for the individual dishes.

Kidney beans	1 hour
Black eyed beans	45 mins
Butter (Lima) beans	$1\frac{1}{2}$ hours
Haricot beans	1 - $1\frac{1}{2}$ hours
Dried peas	35-45 mins
Lentils (whole)	45 - 60 mins
Lentils (split)	30 mins
Chickpeas	$1\frac{1}{2}$-2 hours
Soya beans	3-4 hours
Yellow split peas	1-$1\frac{1}{2}$ hours

Because these times can only be approximate you must test pulses to see if they are cooked. There are two methods and you should use them both. First take up one bean from the pan on a spoon and blow on it for a few seconds. If the skin curls up and away from the flesh it is likely to be cooked. Now, take the bean between your front teeth and bite on it slowly and carefully, testing its softness. Unless you intend pulses to melt into a mush in a soup or stew they should not be soft and falling to pieces. Nor should they be "al dente" as with pasta or green vegetables. They should be tender, without any hard-core at the centre. Tender to the tooth.

To serve one person you will need 4 fluid ounces (roughly 3 ounces by weight) of dried beans. Bring 1 pint of water to the boil in the pot and add the beans. Boil them hard 10 minutes then turn off the heat and leave them to soak for 1-2 hours in the hot water.

Drain the beans and put them into 1 pint of fresh cold water and bring them slowly to a simmer. Simmer them until they are cooked, guided by the times in the table and testing them by the two methods above. Do not add salt to the water. It will make the beans tough. Do not add bicarbonate of soda even if tablets are supplied with the packet or this is suggested on the cooking directions on the packet.

You can always find a good use for cooked beans and, as they keep well in the fridge, you might consider, with a little pre-planning, to cook a double quantity in order to use half of them in a different recipe a couple of days later.

Beans cannot be prepared in a short time so you need to decide upon your recipe in advance and allow the time needed for the beans you have chosen. An alternative is to buy a tin of beans ready-cooked in the tin. These can be perfectly good but cost about three times the price of dried uncooked beans.

Always remember that dried peas and beans absorb water as they cook so that 4 fluid ounces of dried beans will provide roughly the same amount as a tin of cooked beans. A few tins of pre-cooked beans in the cupboard can be a useful way of shortening the preparation time of a pulse recipe if you have forgotten to allow time to prepare the dried variety.

STEAMING

Steaming is a method of cooking by moist heat. It is a fairly slow, gentle method as the food never comes into contact with the boiling water, only with the steam rising from it. You can reckon that steaming will take half as long again as simmering and even longer if the food is dense. It's not absolutely necessary to have a proper steamer with perforations. You can put the food to be cooked between two plates which sit on the top of the pot above the steam. The food then cooks by a combination of the heat from the plate and its own juices and the steam from them. Food, particularly fish, cooked this way retains all its nutrients and is very delicate in flavour.

Master Recipe — Steamed Fish

The fish needs to be really fresh to cook it this way. This method is well-suited to thin fillets of flat fish like plaice but most fish will respond well.

  1 large or 2 small fillets of fish (plaice or sole)
  1 tsp olive oil or melted butter
  1 spring onion (scallion) chopped
  2 plates large enough to take the fish
  A pot of boiling water on which the plates will
    balance

Brush one plate with the oil or butter. Lay the fish on this. If you are cooking fillets then put the skin side down. Sprinkle the chopped scallion over the fish. (If you have no scallion then you could use chopped parsley. Chopped, fresh chives would be best of all.) Place the second plate (inverted) over the fish. Put both plates to balance over the water boiling in the pot. The water does not have to completely fill the pot but there should be enough for it not to boil away during the cooking time. The two plates should make a good seal round the fish so

48

it sometimes works better to use a slightly smaller one on top. A fillet which is roughly $\frac{1}{4}$ - $\frac{1}{2}$ an inch thick will take about 6-7 minutes to cook this way.

But test it after this time. It should flake apart when prized gently with a fork.

Serve this at once. Use a cloth to protect your hands from the steam from the saucepan. Dry the base of the bottom plate before setting it down on the table. You can eat from this bottom plate.

STEWING, BRAISING AND CASSEROLES

These three terms are roughly interchangeable and mean much the same thing in cooking terms. In these methods food is cooked in a pot with a tightly fitting lid at a temperature well below boiling-point. It is not all that different from simmering, except that you use as little liquid as possible in the pot and vegetables and other ingredients and seasonings are added to flavour the food and produce a tasty gravy or sauce during cooking. In this book I use the word "casserole" to describe a flame-proof cooking pot with a tight-fitting lid.

This is the best way to cook the cheaper, tougher cuts of meat, some vegetables and fish. Pre-cooked or partly cooked pulses are sometimes added as well.

As a method it has several advantages. Cooking time is not critical (half-an-hour either way is not going to matter much) and most of the recipes are of the one-pot variety, making the dish easy to prepare. Any vitamins and minerals which leach out of the ingredients during the cooking only get as far as the sauce or gravy and so it is a good way of preserving nutrients in food.

4-6 ozs lamb (This can be a gigot chop, or breast or
neck pieces trimmed of bone and excess fat, then cut
into bite-size pieces)
1 small onion (peeled, sliced)
2 carrots (cut into thin sticks)
3 medium potatoes (peeled, sliced)
1 piece black pudding (1" slice)
1 tbs vegetable oil
1 tbs plain flour
water
salt and pepper
a paper bag
small pot or casserole with lid
1 tsp freshly chopped thyme (this is optional; you
might use $\frac{1}{2}$ tsp of dried thyme)

Put the flour and the salt and pepper into the paper bag. Do
try to use whole black peppercorns which you grind fresh each
time you need it. You will need just a pinch of salt and two or
three twists of the pepper mill. Prepare the meat and vegetables
and chop the fresh thyme if you are using it. Now, heat the oil
in the pot. While it is heating, dry the meat with a paper towel.
When the oil is hot, put the meat (not the black pudding) into
the paper bag with the flour and seasoning. Shake it up and
down to coat the meat with flour. Take the meat out of the bag
and put it into the pot immediately to brown in the oil. (Do not
put in the loose flour which does not stick to the meat.) Brown
the meat on all sides. Not too fierce a heat here, turn down the
heat if the flour shows any signs of burning.

When the meat is brown on all sides remove the pot from the
heat and take out the meat and set it aside on a plate. Place half
of the sliced onions and half of the carrot sticks on the bottom
of the pot. Put the meat and the black pudding (if you are using
it; it is not absolutely essential but is delicious) on top of these.
Sprinkle the thyme on top of the meat and then add the rest of

the vegetables in another layer. Put the sliced potatoes (thinly sliced about a $\frac{1}{4}$ inch thick) on top. Add enough water to reach just below the layer of potatoes. Cover with the lid. The tighter the fit the better. Bring the water in the pot to the boil on top of the stove then place the pot in an oven pre-heated to 180°C (350°F) or Gas Mark 4. If you do not have an oven turn the heat on top of the cooker right down. Simmer for 2-3 hours. Check it occasionally and add a little more water if necessary.

If you like a crispy top to the potatoes take the lid off half-an-hour before serving and brush the potatoes with a little melted butter. Leave them to cook uncovered for the last half-hour. This only works if you have an oven.

Serve and eat it with some good bread to mop up the wonderful gravy.

GRILLING

Grilling is a method of cooking food over an open flame or by radiant heat.   It is the usual method for cooking bacon, sausages, tender cuts of meat and many fishes. It can also be used as a final stage in the cooking of other dishes where you need to brown the top of a previously cooked dish.

The principle aim of grilling food is to seal in the juices of the food by quickly creating a thin outer crust. This demands a high heat initially, after which the heat can be reduced and cooking continues until the food is cooked right through. The lean surfaces of meat and fish need to be brushed lightly with a little fat or oil before cooking to aid the formation of this outer seal. Bacon and other very fatty foods do not require this. With these foods the idea is to allow their excess fat to melt under the heat and drop away into the grill pan.

Only the tenderest meat is suitable for grilling. All of these tender cuts are expensive because there is so much demand for what are known as the "prime cuts." With beef, pork and lamb these cuts come from the middle of the beast, the area that gets least exercise. With beef, working back from the neck, the cuts are known as the T-bone, the Sirloin and the Rump. If you are going to grill meat or pan-fry it (which, along with barbecueing, is essentially the same process) always buy one of these "named" cuts. Loin, side-loin and best-end-of-neck chops in lamb, and chops and the fillet in pork are prime cuts.

Never buy cuts which are labelled "for grilling" or "for frying" because these terms usually disguise the fact that the butcher has gone past the prime areas of the carcass into what is known as "the round" and this is not tender enough for grilling. Avoid like the plague meat, labelled in this way, which looks as if it has been hammered with a patterned mallet or raked with teeth. This method of "tenderising" meat does not work because the meat tends to be cut too thinly or made too thin by this hammering. Ideally, meat for grilling should be three-quarters of an inch thick. Any less and the meat will dry out when grilled. Because a serving for one, cut to that thickness, tends to look rather small, butchers will cut it thinner. They are not helping you by doing this; rather are they effectively preventing you from enjoying a well-grilled piece of meat.

Master Recipe — Grilled Steak

    4-5 ozs of your chosen meat
    a little oil for brushing

Preheat the grill for 5 minutes. Grind a little black pepper over the meat. Never add salt to meat for grilling as it absorbs liquid and makes the juices of the meat "run" so, effectively, preventing a seal from forming. Brush the meat with a little oil all over. Place on the rack of the grill pan and grill it to your taste, turning it once halfway through the cooking time.

Grilling times for prime cuts of the correct thickness:

rare	6 - 7 mins
medium	8 - 10 mins
well done	11 - 14 mins

Lamb chops and pork chops should be cut 1-inch thick

Lamb chops		
	medium	7 mins
	well-done	8 - 9 mins
Pork chops		
	well done	10 - 12 mins

Grilled meats should be served at once; you cannot keep them hot successfully as they tend to lose their juices and continue cooking from the residual heat. While I know that it is tempting to eat chips with a steak or a chop this makes for a rather fat-heavy meal. Try a baked potato, some good wholemeal bread and a salad.

PAN-FRYING OR DRY-FRYING

Despite the name this is really an alternative method of grilling food—when you don't possess a decent grill. You can use it for the same cuts of meat and one or two more which may not be quite as tender. It can also be used for fish (both fillets and whole fish).

Take a heavy frying-pan and set it on full heat for a minute or two then just brush the surface with oil. A teaspoonful poured into the pan and wiped round with a piece of kitchen paper is the best method.

When the oil just begins to smoke a little (about a minute), put in the meat or fish. Keep the heat high and brown the food on one side then turn it over and do the same on the other. Then you can lower the heat and allow it to cook for the correct length of time to be done to your taste.

When it is cooked take it from the pan to keep warm on a hot plate in a low oven or grill. There will be a reddish deposit left sticking to the pan. Pour a little boiling water into the pan. Careful—it will sizzle and boil almost immediately. You will need barely 2 fluid ounces of liquid. Using your spatula, scrape the deposits so that they loosen from the bottom of the pan and dissolve into the liquid. The liquid should bubble and reduce over the heat till it thickens and begins to coat the pan and the spatula. This process is called deglazing. The sauce can be used without further ado as a rich gravy poured over the meat or you can add other ingredients to it to further enrich it. You can use wine, beer or cider instead of the water or add a little cream or lemon juice to the gravy before adding seasoning to taste.

Master Recipe — Liver with Onions and Orange

> 2 satsuma oranges or 1 medium orange
> 2-3 thin slices liver (lamb's)
> $\frac{1}{2}$ small onion (chopped finely)
> 1 dssrtspn olive oil or butter
> ground black pepper

Peel and chop the onion very finely. You can use either 2 satsuma oranges (the small tangerines) or 1 ordinary orange. If you are using satsumas peel one of them and carefully separate it into segments. Cut the other in half and squeeze the juice from it into a little bowl or a cup. If you are using an ordinary orange peel it and separate it into two halves. Separate the segments of one half and cut them in two. Squeeze the other half into a bowl or cup for its juice.

Heat the pan and put in the oil and spread it over the surface. Fry the onion in this until it is translucent but not browned. Do this over a medium heat. Now turn up the heat, make a space by pushing the onions to one side and fry the liver for about two minutes on each side. Remove the liver from the pan and keep it warm. Add the orange juice to the pan and use it to deglaze the pan making sure that the juice bubbles and thickens. Add the orange segments and put back the liver. Heat it through quickly, making sure it gets coated by the thickened gravy in the pan. Serve at once.

FRYING

Frying is a method of cooking food in fat or oil at temperatures between 165-200°C (374-392°F). You can shallow fry (partial immersion) or deep-fry (total immersion) or stir-fry (which is a Chinese technique somewhere between the two).

In recent years frying has had rather a bad press from "health food" enthusiasts who have tended to exhort people to "throw away the frying pan." You would be making a great mistake if you followed this stupid advice which only shows the ignorance about food and cooking of the people who recommend it. Frying is an essential and versatile cooking technique and correctly used does not mean consuming excessive amounts of fat, still less saturated fat, which is the fat that true experts agree is the type on which we need to cut down.

Putting food (which contains water even if it looks dry) into hot fat causes the water in the food to be converted to steam. There is a violent bubbling as this steam rushes out and the protein coagulates. The fat cannot enter the food because of the out-rush of steam and the starches and sugars in the outer layers of the food dry out quickly and caramelise to form a crisp brown outer skin. Clearly, the fat must be hot enough to start this process the moment the food enters the fat. If the fat is not hot enough there is no out-rush of steam, the protein does not coagulate quickly enough and the fat, as a consequence, enters the food and makes it greasy and soggy. If too much food is put into the fat at the same time then even fat at the correct heat undergoes a sudden drop in temperature with the same result as not having the fat hot enough in the first place.

For this reason it is essential to use a fat for frying which can be heated to high temperatures without burning. Vegetable oils like sunflower and corn oil, arachide (peanut) oil and olive oil are suitable. If deep-frying is done properly the oil should not pick up tastes from the food cooked in it. Oil must be strained frequently to remove crumbs and food debris from it as these will burn and spoil the flavour of the next food cooked in the oil. Any oil used for frying will eventually burn or decompose and oils do tend to go rancid more easily after they have been heated to high temperatures. You cannot go on using the same oil indefinitely. When it begins to darken replace it with fresh oil. Ideally you should keep the oil in a fridge between uses.

Shallow Frying

The fat or oil should come halfway up the food to be fried. Many different fats and oils work well for shallow frying but in terms of cost vegetable oils are cheaper. Olive oil gives a wonderful flavour but is too expensive. Butter gives a marvellous flavour but is expensive and burns at a lower temperature than the others and so if it is used it should be mixed with a vegetable oil to prevent this happening too quickly. Any fat left over after frying can be strained and used again but fat or oil used for frying fish should not be used to cook other foods.

Shallow frying is really a safer alternative to deep frying if you don't have an electric, deep-fat fryer. It's not a technique I recommend because it wastes oil and fat but it is a legitimate way of frying frozen breaded meat and fish.

Stir Frying

Stir frying calls for a rather different technique as the oil is nearly always incorporated into the finished dish. For this reason far less oil is needed because you will be tossing and stirring thinly sliced pieces of food which cook very quickly. The design of the Chinese wok is perfect for this method because it allows a small amount of oil to be held in a "puddle" at the bottom and so you get an effect almost of deep frying the food which when it is cooked can be pushed out of the fat up the side of the wok while other pieces slip down into the oil. Most Chinese recipes call for arachide (peanut) oil and Italian recipes for olive oil or a mixture of olive oil and butter. Speed is the essence of stir frying.

1 dssrtspn oil (peanut or vegetable)
$\frac{1}{2}$ lb spinach leaves (fresh)
a pinch of salt
$\frac{1}{2}$ tsp sugar
1 tsp chopped garlic

Wash the spinach thoroughly, shaking off the excess water, and remove the thick stalks. Heat your frying pan (a wok if you have it) to a moderate heat. Add the oil, let it heat up, then add the spinach leaves and the salt. Push the leaves round in the oil over the heat for about 2 minutes to coat the leaves completely with the oil and salt. The spinach will wilt, and when it has done so to about a third of its original bulk add the sugar and the chopped garlic. Continue to stir-fry for another 3-4 minutes. Transfer the spinach to a hot plate and pour off any excess liquid. This is delicious hot or cold.

Deep Frying
There are no recipes in this book for deep frying food. This is because it needs very hot temperatures and a degree of control over these temperatures which you cannot really get without an electric deep-fat fryer. It is also a very dangerous technique and I would rather not have any of you on my conscience.

If, despite my warnings, you feel you must deep fry then you must have a heavy, stable pot. It must be large enough to take enough oil for frying without the oil taking up more than one-third of the depth of the pan and immerse the food completely. The deep-frying pan must *never* be left unattended while in use. You must have a well-fitting lid and a fire-blanket to use if the fat or oil overheats and catches fire. Never, ever, try to move a flaming deep-fat frying-pan. Smother the flames with lid and fire-blanket. Turn off the heat and allow at least 45 minutes covered before attempting to remove the covering.

A general temperature of 190°C (375°F) will cook most foods but may be too hot for larger pieces of raw foods like chicken pieces particularly if they have been frozen and thawed. The outside will brown before they are fully cooked. The standard way of testing the heat of the oil is to take a 1-inch cube of day-old white bread, drop it in the fat and watch it closely. It should sink, rise again and turn deep golden-brown in one minute exactly.

Believe me. Forget it!

ROASTING AND BAKING

These two terms originally meant quite different things. Roasting was a means of cooking meat in front of a glowing fire by radiant heat in free air, usually on a kind of spit. Baking was a method which used an enclosed space which was heated by flames underneath or to the side of it.

The modern oven is a compromise. We talk of roasting meat, poultry and game, but baking fish, bread, pies, cakes and puddings. There is no essential difference between the two methods any more; both mean cooking in the oven without additional liquid.

Meats

It is difficult to roast small joints of meat successfully. It was really a technique kept for large joints. But pieces of poultry and whole, small fish can work quite well.

Vegetables

Some vegetables respond well to this method. Potatoes, beetroots, whole onions can be baked in their jackets, but others need fat or liquid to be successful.

Fish

A small whole fish can be roasted but is usually better baked wrapped in aluminium kitchen foil or greased grease-proof paper.

1 chicken piece (this can be a whole breast, a thigh or
   2 or 3 drumsticks)
1 dssrtspn seasoned flour
$\frac{1}{2}$ teaspoon paprika

Put the flour and paprika into a paper bag. Shake them to mix
the paprika through the flour. Please do not attempt to use
cayenne pepper instead of paprika. You can add a couple of
twists of ground black pepper if you wish. No salt.

Wash and dry the chicken thoroughly, blotting it dry with
kitchen paper. Toss the chicken pieces in the seasoned flour in
the bag. Discard any flour that does not adhere to the chicken.
(If you do not wish to eat the chicken skin then you can omit
this step but do leave the skin on during cooking to protect the
tender flesh from drying out.)

Lay the chicken on a rack over a small baking tin in an oven
which has been preheated to 220°C (425°F), Gas mark 7.

Always preheat the oven to the required temperature when
roasting or baking anything. If you are cooking a small joint
you must know what weight it is in order to calculate the
cooking time. Cook your chicken piece for about 35-45
minutes depending on its size. Because of the dangers of
salmonella chicken must always be cooked right through. Err
on the longer cooking time rather than undercook it. To test if
it is cooked, push a small skewer right through the thickest part.
The juices should be absolutely clear without any trace of
"pinkness." The bones will be loose if you jiggle them about.

Quite a lot of "juice" will have run out of the chicken while
cooking. Unfortunately, with modern chickens, especially
frozen ones, this will be mainly water and a fairly "fishy"-
tasting fat. If you want to make a gravy do, but only use one
spoonful of the "juices." Never try to roast potatoes underneath
the chicken as these watery "juices" will give them a dreadful
flavour and make them soggy.

Cook peeled and halved potatoes (quartered if the potato is

very large) separately. Heat a tin with a dessertspoonful of fat or vegetable oil in it until they are both really hot. Put in the potatoes and shake them around to get a coating of the oil. Roast them on the top shelf of the oven above the chicken. They will take about one hour so they should go into the oven before the chicken piece.

Glossary

Baste—To moisten the surfaces of a food, usually meat, during cooking in order to prevent it drying out. This can be achieved with fat, stock, alcohol, fruit juice or water.

Beat—To mix foods by beating vigorously with a wooden spoon, whisk or fork to ensure full mixing of different ingredients and to incorporate air into the mixture.

Black Pepper—The unripe green berries of the plant "piper nigrum" when they have been dried to blacken their skins. White pepper is made from the ripe red berries of the same plant by fermenting the skins to remove them. The kernel which results is "white." White pepper is more expensive and less aromatic than black. Both peppers should be bought as whole peppercorns and ground in a mill as needed because their flavour is volatile and easily lost.

Blanch—To plunge vegetables (usually green) into boiling water for a short time to partially cook them and preserve their natural colour. Often used as a preliminary step before braising or stewing them.

Blend—A gentler form of beating (akin to stirring) to mix ingredients.

61

Boil—See "How to Cook"

Braise—See "How to Cook"

Carbohydrate—Chemical compounds of hydrogen and carbon produced by plants and used by animals as fuel—starches, sugars, pectins and cellulose.

Casserole—See "How to Cook"

Cheese—A high protein food made from milk. There are literally hundreds of varieties and your diet should contain some cheese regularly. The recipes in this book occasionally call for the following types: a hard "grana" type like Parmesan or Regato, a cheddar type, fresh quark, feta, cottage.

The most useful type for cooking is a hard "grana" type. The finest of these is Parmesan but it is wildly expensive. There are others like the Greek Kefalotyri, other Italian types, and the splendid Irish-made Regato. Never buy these cheeses ready-grated. Buy a piece and grate it as you need it on the fine blade of the grater.

Feta is an eastern Mediterranean cheese originally made from sheep or goats' milk. It is splendid cut into small cubes in salads, and eaten with pitta breads and olives. It should be stored covered in salted water in the fridge and keeps well this way.

Quark is a fresh cheese and must be eaten within days.

I do not find modern "factory" cheddar is very satifactory for cooking; under heat the solids tend to separate out from the fat and liquids. Real "farm" cheddars, properly matured by traditional methods, are much better but tend to be expensive. Buy in small quantities.

Deglaze—Use of a frying-pan after cooking a meat by pan frying. The residues which stick to the bottom of the pan are dislodged and incorporated into a tasty gravy by the addition of a small amount of boiling water, fruit juice, stock or cream to the hot pan and stirring rapidly while boiling to reduce the amount of the sauce and thicken it.

Dice—To cut into small even-sized cubes.

Dust— To coat lightly with flour, sugar or spices.

Fat— See "Nutrition and Your Health"

Flour—Plain white flour is used for general purposes in cooking. Strong white flour for bread-making. Self-raising flour contains a raising-agent and is usually used for cakes. Whole-meal or whole-grain flour is a "brown" flour milled without removing the germ and outer husk of the grain. All cereals, like rice, rye, maize, can be bought ground into flours.

Fry—See "How to Cook"

Garlic—A member of the onion family and a wonderful flavouring in food. Fresh garlic is widely available and easy to use. Never buy or use commercially prepared products like garlic salt, garlic puree, garlic pepper or garlic powder. I think they smell dreadful and taste worse. Fresh garlic is bought by the "bulb" and recipes call for a specified number of "cloves" which are the individual small segments which form the bulb. These should be peeled and the root end and growing tip removed. To do this place the clove on its side on a plate and press down on it with the flat of a knife blade. The tough skin will split allowing the flesh to be removed for use.

Grill—See "How to Cook"

Herbs—Aromatic plants used to flavour food. These are best used freshly picked from the garden but this is not always practical as many are seasonal, and some difficult to grow well in temperate climates. Dried herbs are often substituted but these can be variable in quality and flavour. Freeze-dried herbs are more reliable if you can get them. Fresh parsley, thyme, rosemary and sage are usually available throughout the year. The most commonly used herbs are basil, bay, chervil, chives, dillweed, marjoram, mint, oregano, parsley, rosemary, sage, tarragon and thyme. If you are substituting dried herbs for fresh in a recipe always use less than the amount recommended for the fresh herb. ($\frac{1}{2}$ - $\frac{1}{3}$).

Marinade—A mixture of oil, wine or wine vinegar, lemon juice, herbs or spices used to flavour or, more usually, to tenderise meat and fish before cooking.

Minerals— Non-organic factors in foods, like Calcium, Iodine, Iron, Zinc, etc. Each mineral has a part to play in keeping the human body healthy.

Nutrition—The process by which the body takes in and utilises food.

Olive Oil—The original oil for cooking. Some trees, still fruiting, are over 2,000 years old. The oil is pressed from the fruit of the tree. The best oil, called first, cold-press, virgin oil, has a wonderful fruity taste.

Traditionally the best oils come from Italy and the further south in Italy the better. But some Greek oils are excellent. Avoid Spanish oils as they tend to like their oil slightly rancid.

The thicker and greener the oil looks the better it is likely to taste. Olive oil is high in mono-unsaturated fats and is positively good for you.

Poach—See "How to Cook"

Protein — An essential part of every human cell, they are built up from smaller units called amino acids. When we eat protein rich foods the amino acids in them are absorbed into the bloodstream and carried to the tissues of the body.

Puree—To render solid foods into a mash as in "mashed" potatoes or thick soup. This can be done in a food-processor or a mouli-sieve by forcing the food through a fine mesh. The result is a puree.

Reduce—To boil down a liquid, thus driving off water, in order to reduce it in quantity and intensify its flavour. See Deglaze.

Roast—See "How to Cook"

Roux—See "Rouxes, Veloutés, Sauces and Dressings."

Season—To add salt, pepper or other spices to food to improve the flavour.

Seasoned Flour—Flour to which has been added salt and freshly ground black pepper or other spices.

Shred—To chop finely into thin strips.

Simmer— See "How to Cook"

Soy Sauce—A strong sauce fermented from soya beans and much used in Chinese cooking. "Light" Soy sauce is thin and salty and used as a condiment; "Rich" Soy sauce is thicker, stronger-tasting and used during cooking to give extra flavour and a deep rich colour to food.

Spices—A dried, aromatic seed or root. Those most commonly used in cooking are cinnamon, cloves, coriander, cumin, fennel, fenugreek, juniper, mustard, nutmeg, mace, pepper, sesame, turmeric, ginger, anise, cayenne or chilli pepper.

Steam— See "How to Cook"

Stew— See "How to Cook"

Stir-Fry— See "How to Cook"

Stock—Made by adding liquid (usually water) to the bones and flesh of meat (which may or may not have been browned first in the oven), to strongly flavoured vegetables, or to fish, with added vegetables, herbs and spices. This is cooked slowly to produce a rich-tasting, thin soup which is then strained and stored.

Strain—To separate the liquid from a cooked food, usually by the use of a sieve or strainer.

Sweet Pepper—The large fruits of the Capsicum plant which come nowadays in many different sizes and colours, most usually green, red and yellow. They vary greatly in flavour and "hotness" and only the flesh should be used. Remove the stem and the central core and all the small white seeds which are very fiery. The smaller, near-relative, red or green chilli peppers are often used whole and can be blisteringly hot. Always wash your hands after handling them and never touch your eyes without doing so. Cayenne pepper is made from dried ground chilli peppers.

Vitamins— A group of organic chemical substances present in some foods and which are essential in minute quantities for the maintenance of health, growth and proper functioning of the body's life-sustaining chemical processes.

Wheat Germ—The embryo plant which is removed from wheat grains during the milling process to make white flour. It is rich in proteins, fats, minerals and vitamins and, as a result, is extremely good for you. (So is the germ of oats.) If you habitually eat white bread it is a good idea to take some wheat germ as a supplement. It can be bought in packets but once opened the packet should be stored in a fridge as the oils contained in the germ quickly become rancid. This is why whole-meal flours do not keep well.

Whip—To beat eggs or cream vigorously until they are frothy and thick with captured air.

Whisk—A looped utensil used to beat air into eggs, cream or batter. The act of using a whisk to "whip" these foods.

Breakfast

Nothing has ever seemed quite as ridiculous to me as the fact that people are prepared to stuff themselves full of food just before they go to sleep at night, then not eat anything substantial when they get up, or for another five hours afterwards. This is the height of folly.

It is difficult to eat something substantial in the morning especially if you have not left yourself time to prepare it before you must leave the house. Coffee or tea on an empty stomach creates only a temporary "high" and many experts point out that the subsequent "low" is probably just as marked and question the ability of many people to function effectively, at work or study, under such conditions.

So do make an effort to eat a breakfast. It is no good arguing that you ate a hearty dinner the night before. You cannot slow down the processes of digestion and food conversion or expect them to stop because you are asleep. The energy from that meal, in the absence of activity to burn it off, has been largely converted into "weight" instead. You do not have to eat a cooked breakfast but it should contain a balance of the different food types.

A minimum uncooked breakfast should consist of fruit or unsweetened fruit juice, a wholemeal cereal like an unsweetened muesli with low-fat milk with two slices of good wholemeal bread. If you had the time then one slice of wholemeal bread with some protein like sardines, or cheese, or a grilled rasher, or an egg cooked any way you like, would stand to you later in the morning.

Whatever you do avoid sugary foods or high-fat foods like sausages or sausage rolls or meat pies. Eat fresh or dried fruit and yoghurt instead.

How to Boil, Poach, Scramble and Fry Eggs

This seems like the best place to describe how to cook eggs. One of the main impulses to write this book came from the horrific discovery that neither my own son, nor the daughter of a friend of mine who has spent five years "doing" domestic science at school, could actually produce an acceptable boiled egg. She, at least, could make a passable attempt at a jam sponge and "fairy" cakes.

Soft-Boiled Eggs

Three basic methods produce roughly the same state of "hardness" or "softness" when you boil eggs which are Size 2 or 3. Ignore the classification of eggs as A, B, or C; it does not in practice mean anything. It is physical size, shown by the numbers 1, 2, 3, 4, which matters. Eggs boiled using these three methods are "soft" enough for eating with "soldiers," with firm whites and "runny" yolks.

Method 1 : Place your egg into a small pot with enough cold water to just cover it completely. Place it on the heat and when the water comes to a full boil the egg should be cooked. You will have to experiment once or twice with all of these methods to get them cooked to your own liking.

Method 2 : Put your egg into a small pot and put enough water into the pot to just cover the egg completely. Take out the egg and bring the water to the boil. Now lower the egg quickly into the boiling water and let it boil for 4 - 4½ minutes. The shell of the occasional egg may crack just after it has gone into the water. Don't worry, it will seal itself with a small amount of white forming a bubble on the outside of the crack. If you add salt to the water it will limit the amount which oozes out. Again, experiment once or twice with the exact time, but it will be over 4 minutes and under 5 minutes.

Method 3 : Follow the procedure for Method 2 but boil for only 1 minute exactly. Remove the pan from the heat and leave the egg to stand in the hot water for a further 5 minutes.

Of these three methods I find Method 2 to be the most reliable.

Hard-Boiled Eggs

You might think that there is nothing you could do wrong when you want to hard-boil an egg. There is. Put the egg into cold water and bring it to the boil. From the moment the water boils never boil eggs for more than 8-10 minutes. If an egg is kept in boiling water for 12 minutes the yolk is subject to a chemical change and produces sulphureted hydrogen. Even the freshest egg will then smell frightful when the shell is removed. You have been warned.

If the eggs are needed cold, crack the shells and plunge them into cold water. This prevents the formation of a black ring round the yolks.

Poached Eggs

This method of cooking eggs is shrouded in mystery and complications. Its success is entirely dependent upon the freshness of the egg. The difficulty is to get the white of the egg to huddle close to the yolk in a neat shape. You will read in other books about having the water swirling round the pan at the moment of entry, about the addition of vinegar to the water. Believe me, if the egg is not completely fresh none of these precautions will make the slightest difference. This is because the older the egg the more "watery" the white becomes. The white of an old egg spreads into the water and there's nothing you can do about it.

Method: Break your eggshell and put the egg onto a saucer, into a cup or a ladle. (You will be able to see now how fresh your egg is. The white of a really fresh egg is thick and sits in a sort of heap round the yolk.) Boil about a pint of water in a small pot and add a teaspoon of wine vinegar to it. Never add salt to the water as salted water dissolves some of the globulin in the white.

Carefully tip the egg into the boiling water (you can make it swirl if you like with a quick stir of a wooden spoon). The moment the water returns to the boil remove the pan from the heat. Cover the pot with a lid and leave the egg to stand in the water for 3 minutes. This produces a softly poached egg. Use the three minutes to make your slice of toast.

Use a slotted spoon to remove the egg from the water and place it onto a sheet of absorbent kitchen paper. Tip the egg over by lifting two corners of the paper. This dries the egg. Now put it on top of your toast. Sprinkle with a little salt and freshly ground black pepper.

Some people put the egg into the water in its shell for exactly 30 seconds before cracking it open. I've never seen this make the slightest difference but others swear by it.

Scrambled Eggs

Break 2 eggs into a small bowl and beat them with a whisk until they are well-mixed and "fluffy" and add a pinch of salt. Don't add anything else to the eggs. Do not beat the eggs until you are absolutely ready to cook them. If you are bent on the classic scrambled eggs with smoked salmon slivers, now is the time to prepare the salmon.

Melt a heaped teaspoon of butter in a small pot over a low heat and then add the beaten eggs. Whisk them all the time, scraping the sides and bottom of the pot. The eggs will start to thicken. Remove them from the heat. Now is the time to add another small knob of butter or a tiny amount of fresh cream (and the salmon slivers). Continue to beat them for a minute or two until they are to your liking. They should never be completely set or firm. Turn them out onto a warm (not hot) plate or onto warm toast. Eat at once. You must have the toast ready.

Fried Eggs

I don't like fried eggs. But my husband and son adore them and this is my husband's method. He says it is absolutely the only way to fry eggs. But then he's like that about everything. I have to admit they look lovely!

Heat a tablespoon of good olive oil in a frying pan. He says it "must" be olive oil and it must be a good, fruity tasting one. (See Glossary under "Olive Oil.") In actual fact you can use butter, vegetable oil or even bacon fat.

The heat to which you bring the oil decides the way the eggs cook.

If you like them browned and crisp on the bottom or cooked on both sides then it should be very hot. If you like them glistening white with a bright yellow, soft yolk then it should be only warm.

Break the egg carefully into the oil and fry over a low heat for a soft yolk, a slightly higher heat for a firm yolk. You will see when they are cooked to your liking. (Anywhere between 2 and 5 minutes.)

My husband and son eat them on wholemeal bread with the olive oil from the pan poured over them and a sprinkling of ground black pepper.

Porridge

There is no better breakfast you can eat than a bowl of porridge. Is that a chorus of groans I hear? It is nutritious, high in fibre, and the germ of the oat is positively beneficial for people with a variety of medical conditions. It is also thought to actively reduce the amount of cholesterol in the blood.

Nowadays porridge is remarkably easy to make. Gone are the days of hours of slow-cooking to produce a slab-like cake which tasted like congealed asbestos.

Buy one of the quick-cook brands. They are all called "Oat Flakes" with the word "porridge" somewhere on the packet. Five minutes is all it takes to cook.

Method: Measure 3 fluid ounces of oat-flakes and put them into a small pot. Add 9 fluid ounces of cold water and a good pinch of salt. Bring the water slowly to the boil stirring all the time. The porridge will begin to thicken and bubble. When this happens turn down the heat. Continue to stir. Leave over a low heat, stirring occasionally until five minutes have elapsed. Serve in a warm bowl with a little cream or milk and a teaspoon of sugar or honey.

If you put the 3 fluid ounces of oats to soak overnight in the

9 fluid ounces of water then you need only bring it to the boil and cook for one minute.

Mid-Day Meal

I am assuming that you will eat this away from home most days in a canteen, snack-bar or fast-food restaurant.

The food on offer is likely to be "processed" in one form or another. Do try and stick to the guidelines for eating balanced meals. If you have a hamburger then try to eat a salad or vegetables with it. Failing that have some fresh fruit afterwards. Remember that "packet" soups (soups made from dried powders with added water) can contain large amounts of salt and little else. If you must have them then eat wholemeal bread with them. If you eat sandwiches try to eat those that are made with wholemeal bread and contain "salad," however skimpy.

Things to Cook

Egg Recipes

Most of the basic methods of cooking eggs were covered in the section on Breakfast. One basic method we did not cover was how to cook an omelette.

Omelettes

You will need 2 eggs to make a successful omelette. Break the eggs into a bowl, season them, and beat them lightly. They should not be beaten into a froth and you should not beat them until you are ready to cook them. If you are going to prepare an omelette with a filling then you should always prepare the filling first and keep it warm if necessary.

Method: The perfect omelette should be golden brown on the outside and still slightly liquid, loose, or not fully set, inside. Butter is the best fat for cooking omelettes because it aids the browning process.

The pan, preferably a 7-inch frying pan, should be heated until it is very hot but not red-hot. Drop $\frac{1}{2}$ tsp of butter into the hot pan and swirl the pan to send the melted butter over the bottom. Allow the butter to just begin to brown. If the pan is hot enough it will take seconds. Tip the pan towards you and pour in the beaten eggs. They will begin to set at once. The whole process is very quick. Let the pan return to the horizontal and the eggs will spread over the bottom. Now, add whatever filling you are going to use, spreading it over the near half of the omelette. Pull the top half of the omelette towards you with the spatula and tip the pan so that the runny egg still left on the surface fills this small space and sets. Cook for a very short time more, until there is very little liquid egg on the top of the omelette.

You should, at this point, perform one of those master-chef sleight-of-hand tricks to get the omelette off the pan and neatly onto the warm plate from which you will eat it. You should flip one third of the omelette, from the far side of the pan, back on itself towards the centre and then do the same with the third on the nearside. Now when you put the spatula under the folded omelette and turn it over onto the plate the seam should be underneath. If you cannot manage this, and it does take five times longer to describe than to do, simply fold one half of the omelette over the other and slide it onto the plate. This whole process is extremely fast, two minutes from start to finish.

Omelette Fines Herbes

This is the classic French omelette and only worth doing if you have fresh herbs. These should be tarragon, chives, chervil and parsley. You can make an approximation of it if you can get fresh parsley and chives which are commonly available. For two eggs you will need a tablespoonful of finely chopped herbs. Simply follow the basic method adding the herbs at the filling stage.

Tomato Omelette

 1 large fresh tomato (skinned and chopped)
 2 eggs (beaten)
 $\frac{1}{2}$ tsp fresh basil, oregano or marjoram (finely chopped);
   If you have only dried herbs then use just a pinch.

To skin the tomato put it into a cup and pour enough boiling water over it to cover. Leave it in the water for 30-40 seconds. Stick a fork into it and remove it from the cup. This will split the skin which is then easily peeled away. Chop it finely. As a variation to this recipe add a chopped spring onion (scallion) to the tomato.

Bacon and Potato Omelette

  2 eggs (beaten)
  1 streaky bacon rasher
  1 medium-sized cooked potato
  freshly ground black pepper

Cut the rasher crossways into thin matchsticks. Dice the potatoes into small $\frac{1}{2}$ - inch cubes. Put the bacon into your omelette pan over a medium heat and fry it until the fat runs then add the diced potato. Turn the heat up to high and brown them both crisp. Now pour in your beaten eggs and add a twist or two of ground black pepper and proceed as if it was an ordinary omelette.

Eggah

This is a Middle Eastern omelette and makes a very satisfying meal from two eggs and some emergency cupboard vegetables. There are dozens of possible combinations but this is my favourite.

  2 eggs (beaten)
  1 large potato (peeled, sliced thinly)
  $\frac{1}{2}$ onion (peeled, sliced thinly)
  1 tbs fresh chopped parsley
  $\frac{1}{2}$ tsp marjoram or oregano
  2 tbs chopped plum tomato (tinned)
  1 tbs olive oil
  salt and freshly ground black pepper

Heat the olive oil in your 7-inch frying pan. Fry the onion in the oil until it is golden (not brown). Add the tomato, the thinly sliced potato (uncooked), herbs and seasoning. Cover the pan with a tight lid and simmer until the potatoes are cooked (20 minutes). You could use cooked potato and this would cut down this cooking time to 10 minutes. The sauce will have begun to blend and thicken. Now tip in the beaten eggs and mix them all through the mixture by lifting sections of the potato and tomato sauce with your spatula. Cook, uncovered, until the omelette is set all the way through and nicely brown and crisp on the bottom. Put it under a hot grill to set the top of the omelette and then turn the whole thing out onto a hot plate. If it sticks, it shouldn't but it might, break all the rules and eat it from the pan. Serve with a green salad and bread.

Pancakes

> 2 eggs (beaten)
> 8 fluid ounces plain flour
> 4 fluid ounces milk
> 4 fluid ounces water
> 1 tbs melted butter

Measure the flour and put it in a mixing bowl. This amount of flour is only 4 ounces by weight but because it is very light and fluffy measures more by volume than you would expect. About 7 gently rounded tablespoonfuls are the right amount too. Measure and mix the milk and water. Make a little well in the middle of the flour and tip the beaten eggs into this. Use a whisk to mix them together until you have a thick paste. If you have lumps get rid of them at this stage. Slowly whisk in the milk and water mixture, beating all the time. You should end up with a mixture the consistency of thin cream. Pour the mixture back into the measuring jug.

Heat the frying pan until it is quite hot and then grease it with some of the butter. (Dip a piece of folded kitchen paper into it and rub this over the surface of the pan.) Pour about 2 tablespoonfuls of the mixture onto the pan and tilt it so that the mixture spreads evenly all over the base of the pan. Leave it over a medium heat till the surface of the pancake has bubbles and little holes all over it. Lift the edge gently with a spatula to see if it is nicely golden underneath. When it is, slip the spatula under it and turn it over onto the other side. This will not take quite as long to cook.

Believe me, this all takes far longer to describe that it takes to do. At the first couple of attempts you might end up with more batter in the pan than you need or you might find that the batter is too thick to spread evenly. (This is due to the differing sizes of eggs.) If this happens then just add a little more water and whisk it through the mixture. Cook one pancake at a time and eat it before going on to cook another. You may have to adjust the heat from time to time. This is quite normal and much easier to do on a gas ring than on an electric element.

This amount makes about 10 - 12 pancakes. If this seems too many for you then its very easy to halve the mixture. (Divide everything by two!) Or you could make the whole amount and store half of them for a few days in the fridge. They can be used another day as stuffed, savoury pancakes.

Savoury Pancakes

There is no limit to what you can stuff pancakes with. Just remember that you need both a stuffing and a sauce in which to reheat them once they are stuffed.

Cheese and Mushroom Filling

    5 or 6 cooked pancakes
    2 tbs cottage or Quark cheese
    3-4 finely chopped mushrooms
    1 spring onion (chopped)
    1 dssrtspn vegetable or olive oil

For the cooking sauce: 2 fluid ounces of white, cheese, or tomato sauce. (See "Rouxes, Veloutés, Sauces and Dressings")

Heat a small pan and fry the mushrooms and spring onion in the oil for about three minutes. Mix these into the cheese and season with a little salt and ground black pepper to taste. Put a spoonful of this mixture onto each pancake in turn and roll them up into a cylinder and put into a baking dish. (The lid of your casserole will do fine.) Pour the sauce over the pancakes and heat in the oven for 15 minutes or so. If you have no oven then you can heat them in a small frying pan or a heatproof dish for 5 minutes then put them under the grill for 3 minutes to heat the top. Serve with a salad and wholemeal bread.

As a variation you could use leftover baked fish, or leftover chicken (chopped up) instead of the cheese or even an all vegetable filling.

Egg Sandwiches

The best of all sandwiches, especially in summer.

> 1 hard-boiled egg
> 1 dssrtspn mayonnaise
> 1 tbs watercress, mustard 'n' cress, chopped chives,
>   or spring onion
> salt and ground black pepper
> lightly buttered wholemeal bread

Chop the egg and then mash it finely in a bowl with the back of a fork. Mix in all the other ingredients lightly. Fill the sandwiches.

You can make an **Egg Mayonnaise** with exactly the same ingredients.

Just mix together everything except the egg and the bread. Cut the egg in half lengthways. Spoon the mayonnaise mixture over the egg halves and eat with the bread and a green salad.

The Master Recipe for pasta is in the "How to Cook" chapter.

In Italy, pasta is always eaten as a first course before the meat course, rather in the way that Yorkshire folk used to eat Yorkshire Pudding as a filler before attacking the roast beef.

There is a great deal to be said for this practice because it blunts the appetite so that you do not need the large servings of meat that we expect. After a plate of pasta, always served with a sauce however simple, a small portion of meat or fish with a generous serving of delicious vegetables and some good bread (always served with the meal in Italy) provides a perfectly balanced meal.

There is no reason why you should not eat pasta as a main course and the quantities in the recipes are based on a serving for a main course. If you eat it as a starter then you would need less.

Always prepare the sauce which is to accompany the pasta first because the pasta must be sauced as soon as it is cooked.

Basic Tomato Sauce

This is the quickest sauce to prepare. It is cheap, simple and complements every pasta shape under the sun.

The recipes in this book which call for cooked tomatoes almost always demand Italian "plum" tomatoes, from a tin or jar, which are stronger flavoured, juicier, and richer in colour than those generally available fresh in the shops. An added advantage of using tinned tomatoes is that they are already skinned. When you open a tin of tomatoes pour them into a bowl and chop them up well with a sharp knife. Keep them in the fridge. You will never need a whole tin of tomatoes for a recipe in this book so this is necessary. You must never store them in the tin after it has been opened.

A 14 oz tin of plum tomatoes contains roughly five medium-sized tomatoes which make up about 10 tablespoonfuls when they are well chopped.

$\frac{1}{2}$ tin plum tomatoes (chopped) or
5 tbs of chopped from a jar
1 dssrtspn carrot (chopped fine)
1 dssrtspn celery (chopped fine)
1 small onion (peeled, chopped)
3 tbs olive oil
salt and freshly ground black pepper

Heat the oil in a pot. Fry the onion gently till it becomes golden and translucent. The carrot and celery are optional. (The amounts are the equivalent of $\frac{1}{2}$ a small carrot and a $\frac{1}{2}$ stick of celery.) Add the chopped tomatoes and seasoning. Give them all a stir to mix the oil into the tomato and simmer, uncovered, for about 15-20 minutes. The sauce should thicken and reduce slightly, until a red-gold oil begins to separate out again from a thick, deep-red mush of a sauce. Italians would pass the sauce through a mouli at this stage and then reheat it. It is not necessary unless you hate tomato seeds.

Variations
Add a dessertspoonful of fresh chopped marjoram (or a level teaspoonful of dried) when you add the tomatoes.

Add 1 teaspoonful of fresh chopped rosemary ($\frac{1}{2}$ tsp dried) and 1 paper-thin slice (1 oz) of raw cured ham, cut into narrow strips, when you add the tomatoes.

Add $\frac{1}{2}$ a green, red, or yellow pepper cut into thin strips about three minutes before the sauce is ready.

Add 5-6 stoned black olives (cut in half) just before serving.

Add 1 tablespoonful of fresh basil leaves torn (not cut) into strips. I don't believe in dried basil. I'd sooner add a teaspoonful of a commercial Italian Pesto Sauce for something closer to the real basil flavour.

Meat Sauce

Once you have mastered the basic tomato sauce you can easily make a meat-based sauce to serve with pasta. Use spaghetti or a thick hollow macaroni type of pasta shape with this. This is not the classic Bolognese sauce but makes a delicious substitute. It takes much longer to cook than the basic tomato sauce so be sure to allow for this.

Ingredients:
Add 3 ozs of minced beef or 2 ozs of mince and 1 whole chicken liver to the ingredients for the basic tomato sauce with added marjoram.

Method:
Begin as you would for the basic sauce but when the onions are ready add the mince and the chicken liver (chopped up finely). Fry these until the mince has browned and separated into grains. Keep pressing it with the wooden spoon to aid this process. Season it and now add the tomatoes. Cover and simmer over a low heat for an hour. Remove the lid and turn up the heat for about ten minutes more to make sure the sauce has thickened and the oil has separated out again. Cook the pasta during this final period. Serve with grated Parmesan, Regato or other hard "grana" type cheese. (Buy it in the piece and grate it yourself.) Never buy Parmesan cheese pre-grated in little cartons or jars. I think pre-grated cheeses dry out and lose their flavour.

Clam Sauce

If you keep a tin of baby clams in your emergency store cupboard this is another quick variation on the basic tomato sauce.

$\frac{1}{2}$ tin baby clams (John West brand are cheap and
    good quality)
1 clove of garlic (peeled, chopped)
1 anchovy fillet (optional)
1 tbs fresh chopped parsley
$1^{\frac{1}{2}}$ tbs olive oil
5 tbs ($\frac{1}{2}$ tin) chopped tomatoes
twist of ground black pepper

Heat the oil and fry the garlic gently until it just begins to colour slightly. Add the anchovy and stir, add the parsley and stir, add the tomatoes and 2 tablespoonfuls of the brine (juice) from the tin of clams. Simmer for 20 minutes uncovered until the oil separates. Season. You should not need salt. Stir in the clams without any of their liquid and just let them heat through in the sauce. Don't be tempted to cook them for long or they'll become tough and rubbery. Mix with the pasta and serve. No cheese with this.

The other half of the clams can be stored in a bowl (with their liquid) in the fridge for two or three days, to be added to a fish soup perhaps; or simmered in their liquid for a few moments, drained, then dressed with oil, a little wine vinegar and seasoning, and eaten with a salad and bread.

Pasta with Eggs and Bacon (Alla Carbonara)

A very famous Roman dish, which can be made in the time it takes to cook the pasta. Spaghetti or Tagliatelle is best for this.

> 1-2 rashers of pale streaky bacon
> 1 dssrtspn olive oil
> 1 clove of garlic (crushed)
> 1 egg (lightly beaten)
> 1 heaped tbs Parmesan or Regato cheese (grated)
> 1 dssrtspn fresh chopped parsley
> ½ 500gm packet spaghetti

The Romans would use a bacon called "pancetta." Stretch the streaky rashers with the flat of a knife till they are about twice their normal size and cut them into matchstick pieces. Peel the garlic and crush it with the blade of a knife. Heat the oil in a small pan and throw in the garlic. Fry it gently till it is a deep golden brown, then fish it out and throw it away. Put the bacon pieces into the oil and fry them gently until they begin to crisp at the edges. Take the bowl in which you will be serving the pasta and break the egg into it. Beat it lightly then mix in the grated cheese, the chopped parsley and a good grind of black pepper. Now put on the pasta to cook. Just before it is ready quickly heat the oil and the bacon again. When the pasta is cooked, drain the pasta and put it straight into the bowl with the egg mixture. Toss it thoroughly with two forks then tip the hot oil and bacon over it and mix it again. Eat it at once. If you follow this with a green salad you have a perfectly balanced meal.

Pesto

This is my favourite sauce for pasta, particularly when you are eating it as a starter or a light meal. It has a wonderful smell, a strong, distinctive taste and a marvellous colour. The sauce is based on the fresh herb basil. Until a year or so ago this was simply not available unless you grew it yourself (difficult to get sufficient without a greenhouse), or only available sporadically in limited, select shops. Now it is quite common to see bunches of it for sale in up-market specialist vegetable shops. It is not particularly expensive, just difficult to come by, because it really needs lots of sunshine and does not travel well.

Because it is a little troublesome to make the quantities given will make enough for two servings. It can be stored quite happily for a few days in a jar in the fridge. It can even be deep-frozen and keeps well for months.

> 1 bunch of fresh basil (enough to give you a handful of leaves when stripped from the stalk. If you have some over, put them in).
> 4 tbs olive oil
> 1 tbs pine kernels (nuts)
> 1 clove of garlic (peeled, crushed)
> 1 dssrtspn butter
> 2 tbs freshly grated Parmesan, Regato or hard "grana" type cheese
> 1 tbs cottage cheese or soft goat's cheese
> 1 tbs hot pasta water
> $\frac{1}{3}$ 500 gm packet butterfly shaped pasta
> pinch of salt

You will need your mortar and pestle to make this with any ease. Put the basil leaves, pine kernels, garlic and salt into the mortar and grind them against the sides with a circular motion. This requires elbow-grease. Add the grated cheese and grind only until the cheese is blended into the mixture. Take a fork and add the cottage or goat's cheese to the mixture then slowly add the olive oil a drop at a time, beating it well in. Finally beat in the softened butter. Cook your pasta until it is done. Just before you drain it add a tablespoonful of the water to the sauce and mix it in thoroughly. Drain the pasta and serve at once with the sauce mixed through it. If you are going to freeze some of the sauce then do not add the water.

A substitute can be made using chopped parsley leaves instead of basil, and even walnuts instead of pine kernels. It is not Pesto but a good, if unsubtle, alternative.

It is possible to buy small jars of commercial Pesto sauce. It is no substitute for the real thing and best treated as if it only contained the basil leaves and a little oil. Add all the other ingredients to it because it does not have enough oil, cheese and pine kernels of its own. Use two tablespoonfuls instead of fresh basil leaves.

Pasta Omelette

If you deliberately cook twice as much pasta as you need and make twice as much sauce (any sauce in the book) then you can make a pasta omelette. Spaghetti actually gives the most interesting texture. Simply mix the leftover pasta with the sauce, two tablespoonfuls of fresh chopped parsley and any other fresh herbs that may be lying around, and a tablespoonful of grated Parmesan or Regato cheese with one beaten egg. (Two eggs if they are very small. It is not critical.)

Put a tablespoonful of olive oil in a small frying pan and heat it until hot but not very hot. Pour the mixture into the pan and spread it out evenly. After a minute, turn down the heat and cover the pan with an inverted plate. Cook slowly for about twenty minutes until it is completely set. Then loosen it from the pan. Put back the inverted plate and turn the pan and the plate upside down so that the omelette is on the plate. Use a cloth because the plate will be hot. Then slide the omelette back into the pan to brown the second side for about fifteen minutes or so until it is browned. This is delicious eaten hot or cold. A marvellous luncheon snack, it keeps in the fridge, wrapped in cellophane, for two or three days.

Rice Recipes

Rice is the staple food of more than half of the world's population. There are many different varieties but only one variety is of real concern to us here—the so-called long-grained rice which is sometimes called Patna rice.

In its natural state rice has a husk but this is always removed before you buy it. The rice grain has a brown or reddish surface skin. The "brown" rice which is sold in the shops still has this outer skin; "white" rice has had this skin polished away. Brown rice has a marginally stronger taste, a slightly higher food value (Vitamin B_1 is lost when the skin is removed) and takes longer to cook. It is also very difficult to get the grains of brown rice to remain separate during cooking. I prefer rice to be "dry," with the grains separate, when cooked; not congealed into a sticky cake. Because rice is not going to be your staple food I suggest you buy whichever one you prefer.

There is one other thing you should look out for when buying rice. A number of companies who market white long-grained rice put the words "easi-cook" (or some near equivalent) on the packet. This usually means no more than that the rice grains have been washed after the "brown" skin was polished away. This rice is quite different from those partially cooked proprietary brands which really have been part-cooked and are usually sold to be "cooked-in-the-packet." All rice is easy to cook. The cook-in-the-pack brands are bad value because rice when it cooks absorbs water. This means that you get less rice for your money when you buy pre-cooked brands. They can work out anything up to twice as expensive by weight than the ordinary "uncooked" brands.

Plain Boiled Rice

4 - 6 fl. ozs. white long-grain rice
8 -12 fl. ozs. water

Everyone's appetite for rice is different and there are as many cooking methods as there are cooks. This method works for "uncooked" white long-grain rice if you want it to be served dry with fully cooked, firm, separate grains. I prefer this because the rice is much easier to use for making fried-rice than if it is wetter, stickier and congealed.

All rice is dusty. It needs to be washed immediately before you cook it. Do this by placing the rice in a bowl and filling the bowl with cold water. Swirl the water round the bowl and pour it off without losing any of the rice. Do this two or three times. If you have a flour sieve then you can do it by placing the rice in that and washing it under a running cold tap.

You will need a heavy-bottomed pot with a lid and exactly twice as much cold water as rice. For 4 fluid ounces of rice use 8 fluid ounces of cold water. The amount of rice you use depends entirely upon your appetite.

Put the water and rice in the pot and bring the water to the boil over a moderate heat. Add no salt. Boil the rice until the water begins to disappear. You will see the rice turn white and swell. Bubbles will make little craters in the surface of the rice. (They look rather like small volcanoes or craters on the moon.) This process will take about 10 minutes or so.

When there is no more visible surface water on the rice, but bubbles are still escaping from the craters, turn the heat down as low as you can get it and cover the pot with a tight-fitting lid. Let the rice cook on for 10-15 minutes more completely undisturbed. Do not be tempted to look into the pot or you will let the steam escape. If you have a pot that will go into the oven without coming to harm then this second stage of cooking is best managed in a very low oven.

If you follow these instructions only two things can go wrong. You might forget about it, in which case it will weld itself to the pot; or you can leave it to cook at too high a temperature for the second stage, with similar results.

Serve the rice just as it is or make fried rice.

Fried Rice

Fried rice can be a perfectly balanced meal on its own.

The full amount of cooked rice from the previous recipe
  1 egg (beaten)
  1 spring onion (chopped)
  1 tbs cold cooked peas
  1 tbs tinned sweetcorn kernels
  2 tbs diced sweet pepper
  2 tbs cooked french beans (chopped)
  2 tbs light soy sauce
  2 ozs cold cooked chicken or fish
  2 tbs arachide oil (or vegetable oil)

This works best in a wok but it can be managed in a frying-pan. Prepare and assemble all the ingredients and heat a serving plate and bowl. Most of the ingredients can be gathered over 2 or 3 days, as leftovers, with this dish in mind. Shred the cooked chicken or flake the fish. Heat the pan. Put in the oil. When it is very hot drop in the beaten egg. Let the egg begin to cook. (Count to ten.) It will begin to bubble. Before it is cooked through (still runny on the surface) add the cooked rice. Stir-fry the rice making sure that the egg gets broken up into shreds all through it. If you stir quickly enough and keep breaking it up this will happen without any trouble. Keep stirring the rice until it is heated through then add the light soy sauce. You can increase the amount of this if it seems too little. The rice should become pale brown only. Keep stirring and add all the other ingredients. Keep stirring. When everything is heated through turn the fried rice out of the pan into the heated serving-bowl. Eat at once.

Kedgeree

The Victorians used to serve this for breakfast but it is a delicious way to use up yesterday's cold fish and yesterday's boiled rice for an evening meal. It also happens to be a balanced meal. Traditionally it is made with smoked fish, usually haddock, but any white fish (whether smoked or not) like cod, haddock, turbot, brill, hake, even rock-salmon or kipper can be used. I have even had kedgeree made with salmon, smoked mackerel, or trout.

If you are using left-over fish then you should omit the preliminary cooking and if you are using leftover boiled rice then all you need to do is reheat the rice in a generous dollop of butter added to the fried onions.

The recipe below assumes that you are preparing the dish from uncooked fish and uncooked rice.

> 4 oz fish (smoked haddock or cod)
> $\frac{1}{2}$ medium onion
> 2 heaped tablespoons of rice
> $\frac{1}{2}$ tsp mild curry powder (Sharwoods)
> 1 tsp sultanas or currants
> 1 hard-boiled egg (shelled and chopped)
> 1 tbs chopped fresh parsley
> 1 dssrtspn of olive oil or melted butter
> salt and freshly ground black pepper (to taste)
> $\frac{1}{2}$ pint water
> lemon juice to sprinkle over (to taste)

Pour boiling water over the haddock and leave it to stand for about 4 - 5 minutes. Drain it and remove the skin. Divide the fish up into large flakes.

Fry the onion in the olive oil until it is pale yellow. Stir in the curry powder then the uncooked rice, then the sultanas or currants. Pour in $\frac{1}{2}$ pint water and bring it to the boil. Turn down the heat slightly but continue to boil the rice gently for about 10 minutes. Add the flaked fish and finish cooking for about another 10 minutes until the rice is tender and the liquid is gone. Stir it carefully with a fork towards the end of the cooking time to prevent the rice sticking to the pan. Taste it and season it to your taste. Turn it out onto a hot serving dish and put the chopped egg on top and sprinkle with the chopped parsley. Put a knob of butter on top and serve it with a lemon wedge. Chutney (traditionally Mango Chutney) is a delicious addition.

Salads

Far too often the word salad means a soft, sliced tomato, hunks of soft, unpeeled cucumber and limp, tasteless lettuce leaves swimming in a cheap, bottled vinaigrette dressing. I defy anyone to gain either pleasure or nourishment from such a concoction. The whole point of eating salads is to get the benefit from the vitamins and minerals in the fruit and vegetables and to enjoy eating them. This means that they must be fresh, crisp and plentiful.

Any vegetable that goes into a salad must be thoroughly washed and thoroughly dried. That goes for lettuce leaves as well. If the leaves or vegetable pieces are at all wet then the dressing will not cling to them and will dress the bowl not the salad.

Salads, with one exception, should never be dressed until they are about to be eaten at the table. Not all salads need a dressing. Some fruits and vegetables—I'm thinking particularly of tomatoes and mushrooms—are best served and dressed separately.

Dressings

Americans have a saying that it takes four people to make a salad dressing: a spendthrift to lavish the oil, a miser to hoard the vinegar, an accountant to check the salt and a madman to stir the ingredients.

For a lettuce-based salad those ingredients should be three measures of oil to one measure of a mild vinegar (or a mixture of vinegar and lemon juice), a good pinch of salt, a twist of freshly ground black pepper and optional herbs and spices.

Personally I would not dream of making a dressing with any oils but olive or walnut; both are pungent, fruity, strong tasting and positively good for you. But I accept that they are not to everyone's taste and they are expensive. Other oils, however, tend to be bland and rather tasteless and, as a result, are not really able to master the sharpness of the vinegar. You do not need much dressing. It is meant to cling to the vegetables, not sit in a puddle at the bottom of the bowl.

Do not cut lettuce leaves with a knife. Tear the leaves apart into mouth-sized pieces after you have washed and thoroughly dried them. You can do this by shaking the wet leaves thoroughly to get rid of most of the moisture and then placing them on a clean dish-cloth. Gather each of the corners into your fist and simply swing it round your head. Admittedly this is best done outside because otherwise the walls get rather wet. The only other alternative is to dry each of the leaves separately with kitchen paper or a dish-cloth. It is very worthwhile. Try to buy the firmer types of lettuce like Cos and the curly endives. These latter are now being sold under all sorts of names like "frizzy lettuce." Chicory Hearts and red lettuces like Radiccio should be treated just like ordinary lettuce. They are slightly bitter in taste but none the worse for that.

Green Salad

This should be exactly what its name implies. Mix together green lettuce, watercress leaves, chicory, endive, green herbs (parsley, mint, basil, marjoram), chopped spring onions, slices of green pepper, uncooked spinach leaves, cold cooked (or raw) french beans, mange tout (broken into pieces). You need to eat the equivalent of about half an ordinary lettuce. Eat less of everything else if this seems more than you can manage. For this amount of salad you need no more than a tablespoonful of dressing. So take a teaspoonful of vinegar, three of olive oil a pinch of salt and a twist of ground black pepper and mix them together. Toss your salad in this as you sit down to eat. Eat it before, during and after your main dish.

French Bean Salad

If you are cooking french beans as a vegetable one day, then consider cooking twice the normal serving (8-12 ozs instead of 4-6 ozs) Eat half of them and simply put away the other half in the fridge (covered). Anything up to three days later, simply reheat the beans for about a minute in boiling water then drain them, and while they are still hot, throw in a handful of fresh chopped parsley, a chopped spring onion, and a tablespoonful of dressing with a pinch of sugar added. Serve these as a salad.

Tomato Salad

Tomatoes can be very "wet" which is exactly what we are trying to avoid in salads. For this reason I think they are better kept separate and dressed on their own and served as an "extra."

> 2-3 tomatoes (depending on size)
> $\frac{1}{2}$ small red onion or 2 spring onions
> 1 tsp chopped fresh chives, mint, basil or marjoram
> ($\frac{1}{2}$ tsp dried)
> a pinch of sugar
> olive oil and vinegar

Slice the onions very finely and put them in a bowl. Slice the tomatoes. (You can peel them first if you wish.) Place the tomato slices over the onion. Sprinkle them both with the sugar and about a dessertspoonful of vinegar. Let them sit for two or three minutes. Dribble a dessertspoonful of olive oil over them and sprinkle the herbs on top. (If you are using dried herbs then add them along with the sugar and vinegar.)

Cabbage and Carrot Salad

3-4 tbs very finely shredded green or white raw cabbage
1 small carrot (grated)
½ small onion or 2 spring onions
1 dessrtspn dressing

Slice or shred the cabbage as small as you can and grate the carrot. Chop the onion or spring onions as small as you can. Mix them all together. Add the dressing and toss. Put into the fridge for half-an-hour. This is one of the very few salads which actually improve by sitting in the dressing.

Salad Niçoise

This, with good bread, is a meal in itself.

1 small head of crisp lettuce
1 firm tomato
2 spring onions
2 radishes
1 celery stalk
½ of the flesh of a sweet pepper
1 tsp fresh basil
1 dssrtspn chopped fresh parsley
2 anchovy fillets (finely chopped)
3-4 black olives (stoned, chopped)
1 hard-boiled egg (finely chopped)
2 tbs dressing
½ small tin of tuna fish

Prepare the egg. Drain the tinned tuna fish and flake it with a fork. Chop the tomato and the spring onions, the celery, the radishes, olives, sweet pepper (any colour), anchovy fillets and tear up the lettuce. Put all the ingredients together in a bowl and add the dressing. Toss and eat with good bread. You do not need to butter the bread as the dressing supplies all the fat you need for balance and the flavours will clash.

Rice Salad

3-4 tbs cold, left-over boiled rice
1 oz cheese cut into small cubes
4 stoned olives (green or black) cut into small pieces
$\frac{1}{4}$ sweet pepper (red or green) diced small
1 pickled gerkin diced small
1 tbs olive oil
$\frac{1}{4}$ tsp Dijon (or other mild) mustard
1 dssrtspn wine vinegar
1-2 oz leftover meat, fish, sausage or salami diced small.

Mix together, so that they are well blended, the olive oil, vinegar, and mustard and season with a little salt and freshly ground black pepper to taste. Toss the rice in this mixture so that it is well coated. Add all the remaining ingredients and toss once more.

Potato Salad

2-3 potatoes (of a waxy variety—not "floury")
2 tbs of either mayonnaise (thinned with milk or cream) or vinaigrette dressing
1 dssrtspn of olive oil
salt and freshly ground black pepper
1 tbs chopped fresh chives, spring onion, parsley or dill-weed

Cook the potatoes in their skins until tender. Drain them and put them back in the empty warm pot to dry out just a little. As soon as you can handle them comfortably remove the skins and cut the flesh into roughly bite-sized cubes. Season with the salt and pepper. Pour the oil over them and mix it through gently. If you are not going to eat the potato salad warm, then allow them to cool at this stage. It doesn't take very long, a few minutes. Dress the potatoes just before serving with either the vinaigrette dressing or the mayonnaise thinned slightly with a tablespoon of cream or milk. Sprinkle the chopped herbs over them. If you try to make this dish with a floury potato it tends to turn into a bit of a mush.

Pitta breads are flat and hollow and make the perfect pocket for a whole range of foods. They can be bought in packets in most supermarkets and delicatessen in white or wholemeal varieties. They are usually sold frozen and can be kept for several days in the ice-making compartment of a fridge.

In the Middle-East, where they originated, they are eaten hot. It is a matter of moments to reheat frozen pittas under the grill.

Pre-heat the grill. Sprinkle cold water on both sides of the frozen pitta. Place them on the rack of the grill-pan and put them under the hot grill for about 20 seconds on each side. They should puff up leaving a hollow in the middle. Slit the pitta along one edge with a knife. Stuff with virtually anything which takes your fancy and eat at once.

Two wholemeal pittas stuffed with protein (Feta cheese is good) and salads make a perfectly balanced meal which can be prepared in minutes.

Lamb Kebab with Garlic Mayonnaise

> 1 pitta bread
> 1 side-loin lamb chop
> 1 tsp olive oil
> 1 tsp lemon juice
> 1 tsp fresh thyme (chopped fine)
> 1 tbs Hellmann's mayonnaise
> 1 clove garlic (peeled, chopped)
> $\frac{1}{2}$ green sweet pepper
> $\frac{1}{2}$ small onion (peeled)
> 1 tomato (sliced)
> Lettuce leaves

Remove the bone and any excess fat from the chop and cut it into bite-sized cubes (1-inch square). Cut the flesh of a green pepper and the onion into similar sized pieces. Put the meat cubes with the onion and pepper pieces into a small bowl and add the oil, chopped thyme and the lemon juice. Mix them all together, making sure that the oil and lemon juice coat all the ingredients. Add a pinch of salt and a twist of ground black pepper. Let the meat marinade in this mixture for at least 15 minutes. If you can, prepare this in the morning and leave it in the fridge during the day.

Thread the meat cubes, pepper and onion onto a skewer. (Metal ones are best but if you can only get wooden ones soak them in water first.) Lay the loaded skewers on the rack of the grill-pan and grill the meat and vegetables under a hot grill for about 10-15 minutes, turning them so that they brown on all sides. Do not overcook the meat. It should still be pinkish and juicy inside. You can test a piece by cutting into it with a sharp knife.

While the meat is cooking, crush the finely chopped garlic with the flat of a knife blade and add it to the mayonnaise along with a drop or two of lemon juice to sharpen the flavour. Prepare a small salad with the lettuce and tomato or whatever else you like.

When the meat is ready, heat the pitta under the grill, slide the meat and vegetables off the skewer onto a hot dinner-plate or into the pocket of the pitta. Sprinkle over the chopped herbs and eat at once with the salad and mayonnaise. These can be put into the pitta as well.

You can make kebabs this way with chicken, pork or beef as well. If you are using chicken or pork cubes cook them longer until there is no pink inside. The juices must run absolutely clear.

Small, whole mushrooms can be skewered along with, or instead of, the pepper or onion.

Turkish Meatballs

- 4 ozs lean mince (you need good mince because it is not going to get long cooking. Buy rib or round-steak, minced.)
- $\frac{1}{2}$ small onion (peeled, chopped very fine)
- $\frac{1}{4}$ tsp ground allspice
- 1 egg yolk or white (optional)
- $\frac{1}{2}$ slice bread or 1 dessertspoonful of soft breadcrumbs

Wet the bread with a little warm water then squeeze out all the water and crumble the bread. (If you are using breadcrumbs omit this.) Separate the yolk from the white of an egg. (Crack the shell and break it in half carefully. Let the white drain off into a cup while preventing the yolk from escaping from the shell. It sounds harder to do than it actually is.) A whole egg would be too much for this recipe. You can use the white or the yolk. The yolk gives a slightly richer flavour. Put all the ingredients into a bowl. If you do not have ground allspice then you could substitute ground cinnamon. Mix them together with a fork until you have a thickish paste. With clean, wetted hands shape the mixture into little balls about 1-inch in diameter, into one long sausage shape the same width, or into a flat hamburger shape. Grill the meat on a skewer or fry it in a pan smeared with a little oil. The pan should be hot. Don't overcook them. They should still be juicy inside. (2-3 minutes for small balls, 4-5 for a long sausage-shape.)

Serve as above with pitta, salad and garlic mayonnaise.

You could add some pine kernels to this mixture if you have them and you can vary it by getting your butcher to mince a small side-loin lamb chop for you.

Fish Kebabs

3-4 ozs of any firm-fleshed fish like angler, cod or
   mackerel.
1 tsp tomato puree
1 dssrtspn olive oil
1 tbs lemon juice
2 chopped spring onions
pinch of allspice or cinnamon

Put the olive oil, lemon juice, tomato puree and the allspice or
cinnamon into a bowl. Mix them well together. Cut the raw
fish into 1-inch cubes and place them to marinade in the
mixture for at least half-an-hour. (Longer if possible, even
overnight in the fridge.) Heat the grill and grill the fish chunks
for about 4 minutes on each side. Prepare a pitta and when the
fish is cooked fill the bread with a bed of lettuce leaves, the
chopped spring onion, a sliced tomato and the fish pieces. No
mayonnaise with this one.

Cold Fillings for Pitta Bread

There is nothing sacrosanct about having hot fillings for pitta.
A cold filling can make an ideal packed lunch or picnic food.
Small cubes of Feta cheese with salad leaves and a dribble of
olive oil is very good.

Parsley and Egg Omelette Filling

1 tbs fresh mint leaves (chopped)
4 tbs chopped parsley
2 eggs (beaten)
1 tsp plain flour
1 clove garlic (peeled, crushed)
$\frac{1}{2}$ level tsp salt
3-4 twists of ground black pepper

Place all the ingredients in a bowl and mix them thoroughly with a fork. Cook as if for an ordinary omelette but let the eggs set firm all the way through. Fold it over and place it inside a pitta.

Tuna Fish Filling

    1 small tin ($3\frac{1}{2}$ oz) tuna fish
    1 heaped tbs mayonnaise
    2 spring onions (chopped)
    1 tomato (sliced)
    $\frac{1}{2}$ small sweet pepper (thinly sliced)
    Lettuce leaves
    3-4 stoned olives (chopped)
    ground black pepper

Drain the tuna fish and flake in a bowl. Add the spring onions, mayonnaise, chopped olives and a twist or two of ground black pepper. Mix thoroughly. If you like the taste of a "seafood" sauce (like that for prawn cocktail) then add a teaspoonful of tomato puree or ketchup as well. Place the lettuce leaves, slices of pepper and tomato into the pitta and spoon in the mixture.

If you only have a leftover amount of tuna fish, you can add a chopped hard-boiled egg.

You may have gathered by now that pittas can be filled with virtually anything as long as you have the contrast of texture offered by fresh, crisp salad and some moisture in the way of a sauce or mayonnaise. (This is a good idea as commercial pittas can be a little on the dry side.) Leftover meat or fish can be used up in this way as well. Experiment.

Home-made Pitta Breads

It is not too difficult to make your own pitta bread and there is no comparison between its taste and that of the frozen commercial varieties. You can cook them very quickly under a hot grill or in the oven.

The amounts given in this recipe will make two large ones and three smaller ones. It is not really practicable to make less. You won't have any trouble eating them. If you like you can make three, eat two, and keep one for your lunchbox the following day. Try it with the Egg and Parsley filling on page 100.

> 6 - 8 ozs plain strong-white flour (Jordans make a good one)
> a pinch of sugar
> a pinch of salt
> a little oil (vegetable or olive)
> $\frac{1}{4}$ pint tepid water
> $\frac{1}{2}$ tsp dried active yeast (DCL brand or Allisons)

The dried active yeast comes in small tins which must be sealed after opening with the plastic cap which comes with the tin. It comes in thousands of tiny yellowish-brown balls which must be reactivated. To do this put the water which is at blood temperature (it should feel just warm to your finger) into a cup (which you should warm) first and add the sugar to it. Add the teaspoon of dried yeast to this. The amount is not absolutely critical. Just sprinkle the little grains over the surface of the sweetened warm water. Do not stir them. They will eventually sink and after about ten minutes or so in a warm (not hot) place a thickish froth will form on the surface of the water. This means that the yeast has become active again and is feeding and multiplying on the sugar.

Sift the flour into a warmed mixing-bowl and make a well in the centre of it. Add the salt to the flour. When there is a good head of froth on the yeast add the contents of the cup to the well in the flour and using your hands mix the water and yeast through the flour. You should be aiming to produce a firm but not a stiff dough. If it seems too wet just add more flour, a sprinkle at a time until you get it right. If it's too dry add tiny amounts of warm water. Keep your hands floured to prevent the dough sticking to them. When it seems the right consistency, you should be able to handle it without it sticking to your fingers. Then lightly sprinkle flour onto a flat surface. Now knead the dough for ten minutes.

To knead the dough you roll it into a ball, then use the heel of your hand to push it out and away from you from the centre of the ball. Fold it back over itself, give it a quarter turn and do the same thing again. You can thump it and stretch it as much as you like. Keep doing this (it will take as least 6 - 7 minutes) until the dough feels smooth and elastic. The first time you try this recipe give it the full ten minutes kneading because that way you will definitely see the change in texture and know what to look for the next time you do it.

When its ready, wash the mixing-bowl in warm water, dry it and then use the oil to coat the inside. Put the dough into the bowl and turn it over and over a few times until the oil forms a light coating all over the outside. This will prevent the dough drying out while it is proving.

Place the bowl in a warm place covered with a clean, damp tea-towel or stretch some cling film over the top of the bowl. Leave it for about 2 hours or until it has clearly doubled in size.

Remove the cloth and give the dough a good thump in the middle. It will collapse. Now take it out of the bowl and knead again on a lightly floured surface for a minute or two. Divide it into two or three equal portions and roll them into round balls between the palms of your hands (like plasticene). It's great fun and very relaxing. Now flatten each of the balls out until they are about $\frac{1}{4}$ or $\frac{1}{2}$ an inch thick and roughly the shape of a flattened rugby ball. Dust them with flour and cover them with a floured cloth or cling film. Leave them to rise for hour at least.

When you are ready to cook them heat the grill. Now place one of the pittas on the rack of the grill-pan (the lower of the two sides of the rack). Wet the top of the pitta with water from your finger-tips or a pastry brush. Put the bread under the hot grill. After about two minutes it will balloon up and begin to colour slightly. Remove it from under the grill, turn it over and put the other side in to cook under the grill for about a minute. When it begins to colour the pitta is cooked. When you slice them they should be soft and white and you should be able to slit them into a hollow pouch with a knife.

If your grill is not too good or you are unsure about doing them this way then cook them in a pre-heated very hot oven 230 - 240°C (450-475°F) Gas Mark 8-9, on an oiled, flat baking tray for 10 minutes. Do not open the oven door during this time.

Allow them to cool, whichever way you cook them, on a wire rack.

Pulse Recipes

Pulses is the general name for all ripe, dried, edible seeds of peas, beans, lentils and grams (chickpeas). They are the staple food of large sections of the world's population and are a source of protein. However, with the exception of Soya Beans (which I find virtually inedible), they lack essential amino acids which can only be got from primary proteins. For this reason it is better to supplement pulses by adding small amounts of meat, cheese, fish, fat, or oil to the dish to correct this lack.

The basic method for preparing and cooking pulses has been covered in the "How to Cook" chapter. All dried beans need the pre-cooking described there under "Simmering" before they can be incorporated in the recipes which follow. If you are using tinned, pre-cooked beans then you must, of course, omit this stage.

Turkish Kidney Bean Salad

 3-4 ozs (5 fl ozs) dried kidney beans
 1 tbs olive oil
 1 small onion (peeled, chopped)
 pinch dried chervil
 1 tomato (or 1 tbs tinned, chopped)
 1 clove garlic
 salt and ground black pepper
 extra pinch of salt
 5 fl ozs of the water in which the beans were cooked
 handful of chopped fresh parsley

Cook the beans according to the master recipe. Reserve 5 fluid ounces of the bean water when you drain them. The beans should be soft but not breaking up.

Heat the oil in a pot and fry the chopped onion in it until it is soft and just beginning to brown at the edges. Add the tomato and garlic (peeled, chopped small, then crushed with the flat of a knife along with a pinch of salt), the dried chervil (fresh if you can get it), the salt and ground black pepper to season. Add the cooked beans and 3-5 ounces of their cooking liquid. (You do not want it to be too wet.) Simmer for 10 minutes.

Serve it, hot or cold, sprinkled with the chopped parsley. (You could garnish it further with some very finely sliced raw onion and a few whole olives.) Traditionally it is eaten with hot pitta bread but any good bread will do. If you eat a fresh salad with this you will have a nutritious meal.

Haricot Beans can be prepared in exactly the same way. Because haricot beans have an affinity with tomato you might cut down further on the bean liquid and increase the amount of chopped tomato. (2 tablespoonfuls instead of 1.)

Another variation is to fry finely chopped carrot (1 small one) and a stick of celery (finely chopped) with the onions and change the herb to fresh chopped marjoram (1 teaspoonful,) or dried oregano ($\frac{1}{2}$ tsp). If you do this give it about 15 minutes extra simmering (to cook the vegetables) before you add the cooked beans. This is a Greek way of serving them.

Chick Peas

Indians have a special way with pulses or dals. My son, who may have been an Indian in a previous life, declares that he could "live on this dish!"

5 fl ozs dried chickpeas (Channa dal)
2 tbs vegetable oil
1 clove of garlic (peeled, chopped)
2 tbs chopped tomatoes
1 medium onion (peeled, chopped)
1 dssrtspn lemon juice
a good pinch of whole cumin seeds
$\frac{1}{2}$ tsp garam masala
a small pinch of cayenne pepper
$\frac{1}{2}$ tsp ground coriander seed
a pinch of dried ginger

Prepare the chickpeas by pre-soaking them overnight. The next morning drain them and rinse them. Put them into a pot with 8-10 fluid ounces of cold water. Bring them to the boil, removing any scum which forms on the surface of the water, and then cover the pot and simmer them for an hour. They can be left to cool in the water during the day. They still require another half-hour's cooking.

About three-quarters of an hour before you want to eat the chickpeas, drain them and save about 3 fluid ounces of the liquid in which they were boiled. Heat the oil in a pot and when it is hot throw in a good pinch of whole cumin seeds. They should begin to sizzle and darken at once. After 20 seconds throw in the onion and fry it until it is a deep golden brown. Turn down the heat to low and add the garam masala and the coriander and stir. The oil and the spices will react and thicken. Add the garlic and ginger. Stir. Fry gently for 2 minutes. Add the tomato. Stir well so that it is incorporated into the thickish sauce which now develops. Add the chickpea liquid, stirring all the time. Now add the chickpeas, salt, lemon juice and cayenne pepper. Give a final stir then cover and simmer for 30 minutes.

The chickpeas should be intact but tender. Stir from time to time. Serve with boiled rice or an Indian bread or a pitta. The traditional garnish, which I would serve as a salad, is quartered tomatoes, onions sliced paper-thin and sliced sweet green pepper.

Italian Beans

Italian country people love beans (cannellini: big white kidney-shaped beans) stewed in tomatoes and oil. They eat them along with strong, peppery sausages (cotechino) and their wonderful bread. Any leftover beans will be used as thickening for a vegetable soup the next day. You can buy cannellini in tins and they are very good but you can pre-cook any other dried white bean to use in this recipe. They should be pre-cooked until they are very tender. This recipe cooks twice the normal amount of beans so that you can make soup the following day. If you do not want to do this just halve the quantities.

> 10 fl ozs pre-cooked beans
> 1 clove garlic
> 4 tbs olive oil
> 4 tbs chopped Italian tomatoes
> 4-6 fresh sage leaves (whole)
> 1 tbs chopped fresh parsley
> 5 fl ozs water

Pre-cook the beans till tender or use a tin of cannellini (drained). Heat the oil in a pot then peel and crush the garlic and cook it gently in the oil till it is golden. Add the parsley and the sage leaves. Stir. Add the drained cooked beans, season them with salt and freshly ground black pepper. Stew them in the oil over a low heat for about five minutes. Now put in the tomatoes and stew for another five minutes then add the water—just enough to make a thickish sauce round the beans. Stew for another ten minutes. Serve with bread, an Italian sausage which you have simmered in water for about 40 minutes, and a salad. Do make an attempt to find Italian sausages, either cotechino or luganega. Many specialist Italian food shops make their own. Failing these, any good meaty sausage will do.

To make a soup with the other half of the beans just heat some olive oil in a pot. Sweat a chopped onion, a finely chopped carrot, a chopped stick of celery and a chopped leek in the oil for about 15 minutes over a low heat in the covered pot. Stir occasionally. Add 3 tbs of chopped tomato and stew for another 10 minutes. Add 8 fluid ounces of water, or bean liquor, or meat stock, the leftover beans and 1 medium potato peeled and diced. If you have some spinach leaves or cabbage then cut them up into fine slivers and add at this point as well. Simmer gently for 40 minutes. To serve, toast a thick slice of bread and then rub it gently with a cut clove of garlic. Place this in a soup bowl and pour the soup over the bread.

Tuna Fish and Bean Salad

This is a classic Italian dish using pre-cooked white kidney beans. It uses only a small quantity of beans so it really makes more sense to cook an extra 2 fluid ounces of dried beans when you are preparing another dish. It is another emergency store dish.

    4 fl ozs cooked white beans
    small tin of tuna fish (3½ ozs)
    ½ small onion (peeled, thinly sliced)
    2 dssrtspns french dressing

Peel and slice the onion into paper-thin slices. Put these in water with some ice cubes in a bowl for half-an-hour. This sweetens the onion and makes it less biting in flavour for eating raw. If you use spring onions omit this step. Put the beans, drained of any liquid, into a salad bowl. Season them with salt and freshly ground black pepper. Drain the tuna fish and break it up into large flakes with a fork. Drain the onions and pat them dry on absorbent kitchen paper. Add them, with the french dressing, to the bowl along with the fish and the beans. Toss well. Eat with good bread or a pitta and a small green salad.

Ham and Lentil Soup

This soup, with good bread, is really a meal in itself. Lentils come in three colours - brown, green and bright orange. The first two are whole lentils and are quite large, the last is a split lentil with its outer husk removed. I prefer the green but it is a matter of choice. Lentils cook quicker than most other pulses. It is not necessary to pre-soak them or to cook them in advance but you do need to pick out any little stones from them and wash them thoroughly before cooking. Leave them to sit for 10 minutes in a bowl of water and throw away any which float to the surface.

    4 fl ozs lentils
    1 ham or bacon hock
    1 fl oz barley (optional)
    1 large onion (peeled, chopped)
    1 medium carrot sliced into rings)
    1 leek (cleaned, chopped)
    1 dssrtspn oil or butter
    1 potato (peeled, diced)
    1½ litres of water

Bacon hocks can be very salty and I would advise soaking it overnight in cold water. Change the water once or twice if possible. If you can get the pork butcher to saw the hock into two or three pieces it helps. There is a lot of meat on a hock but you could use a ham bone with the rinds of four or five rashers as a substitute.

    Heat the oil or butter in a pot large enough to take the hock. Sweat the chopped vegetables in this over a low heat for 15 minutes. Put in the cleaned lentils and stir them to coat them with oil. Place the hock on top and add enough water to cover it. If you have it cut into two or three pieces you will need less water at this point. Bring the water to the boil then cover and simmer for 1½ - 2 hours until the meat is really tender and falling from the bone. Remove the hock. The lentils and the potatoes will have made a fairly thick soup by now. If it is still too thin then boil some of the liquid off while the hock is not in the soup. Remove the skin from the hock (it will fall away if it is fully cooked) and take the meat off the bone. Put away half of the meat to use another day or to make sandwiches. Chop the rest into small cubes and return to the soup. Allow them to heat through again. Your soup is ready. It should be fairly thick.

Lentil Kibbeh

This is a delicious lentil dish eaten all over the Middle-East. It can be eaten hot but is even better cold with a green salad.

> 3 fl ozs green lentils (or brown)
> 1 spring onion
> ½ green sweet pepper
> 2 fl ozs fine burghul
> 1 small onion (peeled)
> 1 tbs fresh mint (chopped)
> 3 tablespoons olive oil
> ½ level tsp salt
> a pinch of paprika
> 1 tbs fresh parsley(chopped)
> approx. 10 fl ozs water

Place the lentils in a pot with the water. Bring to the boil then lower the heat and simmer (uncovered) for 45 minutes or until the lentils are completely tender. You may need to add a little more water. The soup should still be wet rather than thick. Stir in the burghul grains and 1½ tablespoons of the olive oil. (The better the oil the better the dish will taste.) Simmer gently for a few minutes then turn off the heat and cover the pot. Leave to sit for 15 minutes. The burghul should absorb all the remaining liquid and you should be left with a glistening mass of lentils and burghul. Heat the rest of the oil in a small pan and fry the onion gently until it is soft and golden. Mix the onion and its oil with the lentils and burghul. Use your hands to knead the mixture until it is smooth. Keep your hand damp with warm water. Chop the spring onion, the green pepper, the parsley and the mint leaves (dried mint will not do) and add half of them to the mixture. Mix thoroughly. Shape the mixture into little balls or patties. Serve sprinkled with the rest of the herbs and pepper and the pinch of paprika. These will keep in the fridge

Vegetable Recipes

This chapter is mainly about cooking vegetables to serve as an accompaniment to other dishes. There are other dishes which are meals in themselves scattered throughout the rest of the recipe chapters.

Preparation

Buy only vegetables in good condition, store them in a cool, dark place and prepare them only when you are ready to cook them. Wash them, even scrub them, with a dish-washing brush if necessary, but only peel them if you absolutely must and never leave them soaking in water. (This preserves the maximum amount of nutrients.)

Cooking

Never overcook. Most vegetables should be served crisp, with a "bite" to them. Root vegetables are the only ones which should be cooked until they are tender.

Green Vegetables

These lose their vitamins and their fresh, appetizing taste particularly easily. Many people who declare that they do not like cabbage or spinach developed their distaste for them by being regularly served with these vegetables grossly overcooked. They need only brief cooking and should always be added to boiling water, never brought to the boil with the water, and can be cooked by brief boiling, by steaming, by stir-frying, or by first "blanching" them in boiling water before braising or stir-frying them. This category includes cauliflower, celery, bulb fennel (even though they are not green) as well as cabbage, spinach, broccoli, peas, french and runner beans, mange-touts, globe artichokes and brussels sprouts.

Root Vegetables

Root vegetables can be baked, simmered, steamed or braised until tender. Carrots, parsnips, turnips, swedes, beetroot, leeks, celeriac, Jerusalem artichokes and potatoes come into this category.

Vegetable Fruits

A miscellaneous category recognised by gardeners to lump together things like courgettes, aubergines, tomatoes, sweet peppers, and mushrooms. Many of these are eaten raw and can be baked, grilled or lightly fried in oil.

Cabbage with Juniper Berries

cabbage
1 small clove of garlic (peeled)
2 dried juniper berries
1 tbs olive oil
a pinch of salt

The amount of cabbage must be gauged by eye as they vary so much in size. You will need a measure of about 20 fluid ounces when it is shredded.

Cut the cabbage into quarters, discarding the damaged or tough outer leaves. Remove the tough central stalk. With a sharp knife, shred it very finely. (No wider than ¼ inch.) Crush the garlic with the blade of a knife then mash it into a paste with the salt and the juniper berries in a mortar and pestle.

Blanch the cabbage in fast-boiling water until barely tender. Depending on the cabbage this will take from 1-4 minutes. The tenderer the leaves are before blanching the shorter the time it will need. Drain it.

Heat the oil in a pot or casserole and when it is hot but not burning add the garlic paste. Fry this for about a minute, stirring and breaking it up all the time. Add the cabbage to the oil and stir it, making sure that all of the leaves are coated in the oil. (This limits vitamin losses.) You can now stir-fry the cabbage until it is piping hot and serve at once or, if you are using the oven to cook something else, put it into a lidded casserole, tightly covered, to heat through in the oven. It will need 10-15 minutes heating in the oven depending on the oven temperature. This goes well with all kinds of meat dishes—pork, beef, lamb, poultry or meaty sausages like bratwurst.

Variations: If you leave out the garlic paste and use a dessertspoonful of fresh chopped parsley this method can be used with cauliflower florets, brussels sprouts, broccoli, french or runner beans, celery, mange-tout.

Spinach

There are two schools of thought about the cooking of spinach: the first says that it should be cooked in a pot with only the water which clings to the leaves after they have been washed; the second says that it should be first blanched in a pot of boiling water, drained thoroughly, then braised or stir-fried with butter or a little cream. The first method preserves every last vitamin in the spinach and produces a very strong flavour; the second loses some of the water soluble vitamins but is milder in taste. I suggest you try both.

Deep-frozen spinach contains vast amounts of frozen water and must be thawed completely then squeezed dry before cooking. Proceed then as for fresh spinach.

Green Beans

This group includes runner beans, french beans, mange-touts, shelled broad beans and peas. The methods of cooking all of these are similar and the same herbs and flavourings have an affinity for all the vegetables in the category.

If you choose young vegetables to start with they need very little cooking, not much more than 3-5 minutes in fast-boiling water. Drain them, return them to the pot with a little butter, oil or cream. Stir to coat the beans then serve sprinkled with seasoning and chopped herbs.

Variation: For french or runner beans omit the butter, oil or cream and substitute a tablespoonful of basic tomato sauce as for pasta.

For shelled peas and young, tender broad beans grill a slice of streaky bacon slowly until it is very crisp. Crumble it and add to the pot with a little cream. Stir and heat through and serve at once.

Broccoli and Cauliflower

For a serving you will need half a small cauliflower, ½lb by weight of the big green broccoli (calabrese), and about 6-8 ozs by weight of purple sprouting broccoli. Remove the thick central stalk of cauliflower and calabrese and break the head into small florets. Plunge these into fast-boiling water for about 5 minutes. Purple sprouting broccoli will need only 3 minutes and you should eat the leaves as well. These vegetables should be served still crisp, with a bite in them. Drain them and shake out the excess water. If you are serving them with a dish which has its own sauce then serve them just as they are without further ado. If not try the variations below.

Variations: Return the cooked vegetable to the pot and stir-fry as suggested in the variations for cabbage with oils and herbs.

Grease a small baking-dish. Arrange the hot vegetable in this and sprinkle with a tablespoonful of grated cheese of the hard grana type sprinkled with a few drops of olive oil or butter. Put in the oven until the cheese has melted and browned slightly. (You could do this under a low grill.)

Turnip, Swede and Parsnip

These three root vegetables can be treated in the same way. Peel them, cutting away the tough tops and bottoms. With all of these you are better buying the smaller vegetables even though the huge ones may be the same price. Big parsnips need their central core cut away. (Just cut them in half lengthways and the core is the slightly different textured part which runs the full length of the root.) Cut them into even-sized pieces, small ones if you are in a hurry, put them into a pot of cold water over a high heat and bring it to the boil. Turn down the heat immediately and simmer them until they are tender. Drain them, return them to the dry pan and let them steam over a low heat for a couple of minutes to dry out. Mash them thoroughly with a potato-masher and then mix in a tablespoonful of cream and a little salt and pepper. Serve at once sprinkled with chopped chives, a little chopped crispy bacon or chopped parsley.

Variation: Instead of mashing the cooked vegetables fry them in a little butter or olive oil. This is also a good way to reheat left-over mashed turnip. In fact if you have some leftover mashed potato then mix the two of them together before frying them. This works just as well if you mix left-over cabbage with mashed potato.

Baked Potatoes

Choose larger, firm potatoes and wash them and scrub them thoroughly using a dish washing-up brush. Select potatoes with as few flaws on the skin as possible. Dry them well and puncture the skins with a fork or skewer. (This is important. If you do not do this they might explode.) Golden Wonders bake extremely well if you can get them. Place them on a rack in the top of a pre-heated oven, 230°C (450°F), Gas Mark 8 for an hour. You can cook them at a lower temperature but they will take slightly longer and will not have that lovely crisp, crackly skin which is so good to eat. Take a sharp knife and cut a cross in the top of each potato. Press down firmly with your fingers on each quarter and they will open slightly. Put a spoonful of cottage, cream, or quark cheese mixed into a paste with chopped chives, mint or parsley into the opening and serve at once.

Italian Fried Potatoes

These are actually much nicer than chips if a little more complicated to prepare. They are best made with freshly boiled potatoes. You can use left-over potatoes but they will not have as good a flavour. Boil two or three potatoes in their jackets and peel and quarter them while still hot.

Put 1-2 tablespoonfuls of olive oil in a frying pan and heat it. Add the potatoes and fry until golden-brown all over. Don't turn them over too much. Let them brown on one side first then turn them over onto each side in turn. Serve sprinkled with fresh, chopped parsley.

Potatoes with Milk and Garlic

Peel and chop a small clove of garlic. Crush it with the flat of a knife. Grease a small casserole with butter or olive oil. Peel three or four potatoes and slice them very thinly. Layer these in the casserole with a little garlic and some chopped parsley. Pour enough creamy milk into the casserole to reach just below the top layer of potatoes. Cover and cook in a pre-heated oven at 220°C (425°F), Gas Mark 7, for about 45 minutes or until the potatoes are soft and tender.

Boiled Mashed Potatoes

You need a "floury" potato for this dish, Kerr's Pinks or Golden Wonders. Boil three or four potatoes in their jackets until tender. Drain them and return them to the pot over a very low heat for a few minutes to dry them out. Place a clean tea-towel over them to gather the steam. Peel off the skins. Cut the potatoes into quarters and place them in the pot with milk and butter. Heat this over a medium heat till the milk begins to bubble. Then mash the potatoes thoroughly with a potato masher and serve them at once.

Vegetable Soups

It is possible to use potatoes and onions as a simple base for vegetable soups. I give the recipe for a carrot soup made in this way, but by experimenting with other vegetables, even mixtures of vegetables, using this basic method you can ring the changes.

It is not practicable to make just enough soup for a single serving, nor is it necessary, as soups keep well in a fridge for a few days. The knack with this method is to keep the amounts of the basic ingredients the same always and to increase or decrease the amount of the main ingredient until you arrive at a taste which you like.

Carrot Soup

1 tbs butter
4 fl oz chopped onion
4 fl oz diced potato
16 fl oz diced carrot
20 fl oz water or meat stock

Peel, chop, dice and measure each of the vegetables in turn. You should dice the potatoes and carrots into about half-inch cubes so that there isn't a lot of space between the pieces when you measure them in the measuring jug. This method works not on weights but on the ratio between the ingredients of 1 part onion, 1 part potato to 4 parts main ingredients and 5 parts of liquid.

Melt the butter in a heavy bottomed pot and add all the onion, potato and carrot and season them to taste with salt and freshly ground black pepper. Turn them to ensure that they are all coated with the butter. "Sweat" the vegetables in the pot, covered, over a low heat until they are just tender. Sweating means no more than that they cook gently in the butter and their own steam and juices. It should be a gentle process. You are not trying to brown them or fry them. It will take ten to fifteen minutes. Add the liquid and bring it just to the boil before turning down the heat and simmering the soup gently until the vegetables are completely cooked. The potatoes give the soup its body, thickening it as they disintegrate. The length of time the soup takes to cook depends on the size of the vegetable dice—smaller pieces of vegetable take less time to cook through.

Use your mouli-sieve over a large bowl to purée the soup. A degree of elbow grease is necessary here. Return the soup to the pot to reheat it gently. Do not boil it. Serve sprinkled with some freshly chopped parsley. A spoonful of cream gives that little extra smoothness.

It is not absolutely essential to mouli-sieve the vegetables at all. Some people prefer it just as a broth with vegetables. If you prefer this then take more care when preparing the vegetables, chopping them evenly and neatly.

To make larger quantities for a party just scale up the quantities while keeping the ratios the same.

Braised vegetables with cheese and potatoes

This is a simple, economical and balanced one-pot meal.

> potato (1 very large, 2-3 medium, 5-6 small) peeled, sliced
> $\frac{1}{2}$ medium onion (peeled and sliced)
> 1 carrot (peeled and sliced)
> 1 tbs chopped tomatoes (or leftover basic tomato sauce)
> 1 tbs olive oil
> $1\frac{1}{2}$ tsp chopped, fresh thyme, oregano or rosemary
> 2 oz cheese (cheddar, gruyere, mozzarella)
> freshly ground black pepper
> 1 tbs breadcrumbs

Oil the bottom and sides of a small oven-proof baking dish with about half of the olive oil. Layer the sliced potatoes ($\frac{1}{4}$ inch slices), onions, tomato and cheese (grated), seasoning each

119

layer as you go with salt, pepper and a sprinkle of fresh herbs. End with a layer of cheese. Sprinkle the breadcrumbs over the top and dribble the remaining oil over these. Cover tightly and bake in a pre-heated, hot oven at 200°C (400°F) Gas Mark 6, for about 30 minutes. Remove the lid and bake for a further 15 minutes to brown and crisp the top. Serve with a salad and good bread.

Potato and Black Pepper

2 leftover boiled potatoes (peeled, diced into $\frac{1}{2}$ inch cubes)
1tbs vegetable or olive oil
pinch of salt
$\frac{1}{2}$ tsp freshly ground black pepper
1 tbs fresh chopped parsley

Boil two extra potatoes in their jackets the day before you intend to cook this dish. Let them cool in their jackets in the refrigerator. Peel them and cut them into $\frac{1}{2}$ inch cubes just before you intend to cook this dish.

Heat the oil in your frying pan over a medium heat then put in the potato cubes and stir them around to coat them with the oil. Sprinkle the salt over them. Cover the potatoes and let them heat through for about 5 minutes, giving them a quick stir now and again. Remove the lid and sprinkle over the black pepper and stir it in. Continue to cook for a further 3 minutes, uncovered this time. They should be beginning to brown slightly by now. Sprinkle the chopped parsley over them, stir once more, and serve hot. These potatoes go very well with the Indian-style pork sausages on page 140.

Fish Recipes

If the nearest you have ever come to a fish is a battered fish-finger or a bread-crumbed fillet there is a real culinary voyage of discovery awaiting you. Only a tiny fraction of the edible fish species arrive on the fishmonger's slab in this country.

The table below gives a broad classification of the commoner fish types. The classifications are made with an eye to cooking methods rather than scientific accuracy.

GUIDE TO FISH TYPES	
SEA FISH	FRESHWATER FISH

Flat White:
    Plaice, Sole, Dabs,
    Turbot, Brill, Halibut,
    Witch, Ray
 	
Round White:
    Cod, Pollack, Bass,
    Bream, Whiting,
    Hake, Ling, Angler,
    Mullet, (Grey, Red),
    Gurnard, John Dory,
    Rock
 	
Oily: Herring, Mackerel,
    Sardines, Anchovy,
    Pilchards, Tuna
    Sprats (Whitebait)
	Oily (Game):
	    Salmon (fresh),
	    Salmon (farmed),
	    Brown Trout (fresh)
	    Rainbow Trout
	    (farmed) Sea (White)
	    Trout
	
	Coarse: Perch
	    Roach
	    Carp
	    Pike
	    Eel

SHELLFISH, MOLLUSCS and CEPHALOPODS	
Lobster, Crayfish, Prawns, Dublin Bay Prawns, Shrimps Oysters, Scallops, Mussels, Whelks, Cockles, Clams, Periwinkles, Squid, Edible Crabs, Sea Urchins	

COOKING FISH

There are almost as many ways of cooking fish as there are
varieties of fish in the sea. But in the end they all come down to
five or six basic methods.

Boiling

In a word—Don't! Despite the fact that you will come across
recipes for such delights as "Boiled" Cod this method is only
suitable for making fish stock when the object of the exercise is
to get the flavour out of the fish and into the water.

Poaching

This is the fishy equivalent of gentle simmering (See "How to
Cook") and the rules apply. Suitable for a variety of fish as
long as you can guarantee its freshness. This is necessary
because it is going to be eaten rather plain without the benefit
of fancy sauces or accompaniments.

Frying

Fish steaks, fillets and small, whole fish can be shallow fried. It
is usual to coat the fish in seasoned flour, breadcrumbs, or
crushed oatflakes before cooking them this way. Drain them
on absorbent kitchen paper before serving.

Grilling

Whole fish with their skins still intact, especially those
classified as "oily," respond well to grilling. Always slash the
thickest part of the fish with a sharp knife and brush with oil to
help it cook evenly and to prevent it drying out during cooking.

The grill should be allowed to heat up before you put the fish under it. Cook on one side until the skin is crisp and browned. Turn the fish over carefully with a spatula or fish slice and cook the other side. An average sized fish cooked this way will take between 4 and 7 minutes per side depending on their thickness.

Cutlets and fillets are a little trickier. Whole fish can be placed on a rack under the grill but cutlets and fillets, because they are not completely covered and so held together by skin, can break apart if they are cooked this way. They should be placed directly onto the oiled flat bottom of the grillpan without a rack. (Make sure that the pan is clean first.) Cutlets with a central bone can be tested to see if they are cooked by seeing if this bone moves easily away from the flesh. Cutlets and fillets do not need to be turned during cooking and will take about ten minutes to cook.

Kippers (smoked herrings) are an exception to this rule as they should be cooked on a rack, skin side up, and do not need turning during cooking.

Traditionally oily fish is served with something which counteracts the oiliness. It can be as simple as lemon juice or a sharp fruit sauce like apple or gooseberry. Creamed horseradish sauce is good with smoked fillets of trout and mackerel.

Baking

Fish can be wrapped in oiled greaseproof paper or kitchen foil and baked in the oven. It is often laid on a bed of fresh, aromatic herbs (basil, parsley, thyme, marjoram) or a sprig of the herb can be inserted in the cavity of the fish with a little oil or butter and seasoning.

Braising and Stewing

This is a good way to produce one-pot fish dinners by putting a layer of partially cooked vegetables in the bottom of the pot with a little liquid. The fish is placed on top of this layer and the pot is tightly covered and cooked in the oven.

Steaming

This was fully covered in the "How to Cook" chapter. Excellent for really fresh fish and very easy to do.

Cooking Times for Fish

There are extremely complicated rules for measuring the thickness of fish and then calculating the time it will take to cook. All you really need to remember is that fish cooks quite quickly and becomes dry and very nasty when overcooked.

When raw, the flesh of fish has a translucent look and is firmly attached to the bones and skin. When cooked the flesh becomes opaque, firmer, parts easily from the bones and the skin and separates into flakes if you ease it apart with the prongs of a fork or the tip of a knife.

Fish Soup

A very simple recipe which cooks in about 15 minutes. It is better if you use more than one kind of fish. The famous fish soups of the Mediterranean can use up to 10 different varieties including shellfish. This recipe is not on that scale but benefits in flavour if you have a white and an oily fish. If you dislike skin then ask the fishmonger to skin it for you.

 4 tbs olive oil
 $\frac{1}{2}$ kilo (1 lb) fish
 12 fl ozs water or fish stock
 $\frac{1}{2}$ small onion (peeled, chopped)
 3 fl ozs chopped tomatoes
 1 small clove garlic (peeled)
 1 tbs fresh chopped parsley or dill

Choose a pot large enough to take all the fish in one layer. Heat the oil in the pot. Put in the onion and cook gently until transparent not browned. Chop and add the garlic to cook until it is light gold in colour. Add the parsley or dill and turn it over once or twice in the oil. Add the liquid. (You might use cider or white wine as well as water, or stock, or a mixture.) Let it heat up, not boil, then add the tomatoes and juice. Cook gently, uncovered, for about six minutes, stirring occasionally. Add the fish, a pinch of salt and a good grind of black pepper. Cover the pot, turn down the heat so that it barely simmers and cook for 10-12 minutes. This amount will give you about 3-4 bowls of delicious soup. It will keep well, covered, for a day or so in the fridge.

Variation: Omit the liquid and reduce the amount of fish to 6 ozs. (This can be a whole fish; if so, turn it once during the cooking time.) This gives you a delicious stew.

Whether you cook this recipe as a soup or a stew you need a really good bread to mop up the juice.

Greek Style Fish Stew with Vegetables

2-3 medium potatoes (sliced)
2 dessertspoons olive oil
1 small onion (peeled, sliced)
1 tbs lemon juice
1 large carrot (peeled, chopped)
4 fl ozs water
1 stalk celery (chopped)
handful of chopped parsley
1 fillet or cutlet of fish (6 ozs)

Put 1 dessertspoonful of the oil and the water into a pot or casserole. Bring to the boil. Put in the potatoes, onion, carrot and celery and allow to return to the boil. Reduce the heat and simmer for 15 minutes until the vegetables are becoming tender. Meanwhile, skin and cut the fish into bite-sized pieces. Place the fish on top of the tender vegetables. Add the second dessertspoonful of oil and the lemon juice. Cover and cook slowly until the fish is opaque and flakes easily (10-15 minutes). Serve on a hot plate with a handful of chopped parsley sprinkled over it. A little more lemon juice can be squeezed over it too.

Vegetables and Fish

Some vegetables are better suited to accompany fish than others. Strongly flavoured vegetables like cabbage, brussels sprouts, turnips, swedes, beetroot, and broccoli tend to overwhelm the delicate flavour of the fish and most people avoid using them for this reason.

Small amounts of celery, bulb fennel, or carrots are fine. Mushrooms, tomatoes, leeks, spinach, onions, green and red peppers, peas, french and runner beans, artichokes and potatoes go well with fish.

Fresh herbs which have an affinity with fish are basil, marjoram, tarragon, parsley, dill-weed, fennel leaves and bay.

Fish Cakes

People tend either to adore or to loath fish cakes but that is because they have usually tasted only the commercial types. There is no need to use leftover fish to make fish cakes, but it is a good way to use up cooked fish of all kinds. They can also be made out of some of the contents of the emergency store cupboard, from a small tin of tuna fish and a packet of dried, instant potatoes. Try buying a double quantity of fresh fish sometime and use half of it to make fish cakes which will keep well for two or three days in a fridge. They are particularly nice with hot toast and grilled tomato at breakfast time.

> 6 ozs cooked fish (poached or steamed) or
> $3\frac{1}{2}$ oz. tin of tuna
> 2-3 heaped tablespoons of boiled, mashed potato (or instant)
> 1 tsp chopped capers or 1 chopped spring onion
> 1 tbs fresh chopped parsley or chives (not dried herbs)
> 1 egg (beaten)
> 1 tbs plain flour
> 2-3 tbs dried breadcrumbs
> salt and ground black pepper

Remove any skin or bone from the fish and flake the flesh. (If you are using tinned tuna then drain the liquid or oil from the tin first.) Blend the fish well into the mashed potatoes together with the capers or scallions and the fresh herbs and seasoning. Form this mixture into cakes about $1-1\frac{1}{2}$ inches thick.

Dip the cakes first into the flour (all over), then into the beaten egg (all over) and finally into the dried breadcrumbs. Never use the bright orange commercial breadcrumbs. Make your own by crumbling stale bread finely and then drying it on a plate or in a bowl in a barely hot oven.

Shallow fry the fish cakes in hot oil in a frying pan until crisp on both sides.

Fish Baked in Paper or Foil

    1 dssrtspn olive oil or butter
     6 ozs fish
    1 heaped tsp fresh chopped herbs
        (marjoram, parsley, or tarragon)
    Enough foil or greasproof paper to make a loose
        parcel for fish

Lay the paper or foil out flat. Brush with the oil or melted
butter. Wash and dry the fish and lay it in the centre of the
papcr or foil. Sprinkle the herbs over the fish if you are using a
fillet, cutlet or tailpiece or place them in the cavity if you are
using a whole fish. Fold the paper or foil up around the fish,
loosely enough to leave a cavity above the fish. Make sure it is
well sealed. It is actually easier to achieve this with foil.

Bake in the oven at 160°C (325°F), Gas Mark 3. Small fillets
or whole fish will take 10-14 minutes. Thicker cutlets or larger
whole fish will need 15-20 minutes. Serve by sliding out of the
parcel onto a hot plate. Do not lose the juices in the parcel as
these are your sauce. Garnish with a small sprinkling of herbs
or a wedge of lemon.

SUITABILITY OF FISH FOR COOKING METHODS

	BAKE	STEAM	POACH	FRY	STEW	GRILL
PLAICE	✓	✓		✓		✓
SOLE	✓	✓		✓		✓
DABS	✓	✓				✓
TURBOT	✓	✓	✓		✓	✓
BRILL	✓	✓	✓			✓
HALIBUT	✓	✓	✓		✓	
WITCH	✓	✓		✓		✓
RAY	✓	✓	✓	✓	✓	
COD	✓		✓		✓	
POLLACK	✓		✓		✓	
BASS	✓	✓			✓	✓
BREAM	✓	✓				✓
WHITING	✓	✓		✓		
HAKE	✓	✓	✓		✓	
LING	✓		✓		✓	
ANGLER	✓				✓	
MULLET	✓	✓	✓		✓	
GURNARD	✓			✓	✓	✓
JOHN DORY	✓			✓		✓
ROCKFISH	✓		✓		✓	
MACKEREL	✓			✓		✓
HERRING	✓			✓		✓
SPRATS				✓		
SALMON	✓	✓	✓			✓
TROUT	✓	✓		✓		✓
EEL			✓	✓	✓	

Meat Recipes

The recipes in this section are all based on relatively cheap cuts of meat. You will find recipes which contain meat in other sections as well as in the "How to Cook" chapter. This section should be read in conjunction with the chapters on "How To Cook" and "Nutrition and You."

Do remember that you should eat both "oily" fish and liver at least once a week because each of these foods contains nutrients which are essential to your bodily health.

Irish Stew

The basic method of cooking this dish is similar to that for many other simple stews. The meat is not "browned" first as it would be for a hot-pot and so the juices are not sealed into the meat but allowed to leach out and flavour the other ingredients which always contain a starchy, absorbent food like potatoes or beans.

> 4 ozs lamb (gigot, neck or breast)
> 1 small onion (peeled, sliced)
> 2-4 potatoes (peeled, sliced)
> 3 fl ozs water
> 1 tsp fresh, chopped thyme
> 1 tbs freshly chopped parsley
> salt and freshly ground black pepper

Lay the sliced onions and half the potatoes (cut into thick slices) on the bottom of the casserole in separate layers. (Onions on the bottom.) Remove excess fat from the meat and add the meat and the thyme to the pot next. Season. Sprinkle half the chopped parsley over the meat then add the rest of the potatoes on top. Sprinkle with the rest of the parsley. Pour in the water down the side. Cover with a tightly fitting lid. If you feel that your lid isn't making a good seal then use aluminium foil to make a cover and then put the lid on over this. Bring to the boil on top of the cooker then put into a pre-heated oven at 120°C (275°F), Gas Mark 1-1½ for 2-3 hours. The time depends upon the tenderness of the meat and the actual temperature of your oven. It is not critical. Test it after 2 hours.

Variation: Buy a lamb shank. Remove the tough outer sheath round the muscles with a knife and rub ½ teaspoon of paprika which has been made into a paste with a crushed clove of garlic into the meat. Omit the onion and parsley from the recipe above and add instead 1 tablespoonful of chopped tomato and a small sprig of fresh rosemary. (½ tsp dried.) Cook for the same length of time as Irish Stew. This is a Turkish recipe.

Variation: Dublin Coddle is much the same dish but uses bacon and pork sausages instead of lamb. Use 2 ozs of bacon bits (or the left-over bacon from the bacon hock used to make lentil soup) and 2 pork sausages.

Chinese Red-Stewed Pork

        1 pork (not bacon) hock
        ½ pint boiling water
        4 tbs thick (rich) Soy sauce
        2 tsp brown sugar
        1 tsp dried powdered ginger
            (or 3 ¼ inch thick slices fresh root)
        1 tbs rice wine (or 1 tbs wine vinegar and 1 tbs water
            mixed)

Place the hock and the water in a pot. Bring the water to the boil and add all the other ingredients. Turn down the heat to very low and cover tightly. Simmer for 2-3 hours. You should turn the hock over in the liquid every half-an-hour or so that it colours evenly. The meat should be falling off the bone when it is done. (It can equally well be cooked in a very low oven 120°C (250°F), Gas Mark 1.)

Remove the meat and the skin from the hock. Cut enough meat into thin slices and serve it, with a spoonful of the stock, stir-fried vegetables and plain boiled rice. The skin is delicious as well. (Soft and jellied.) You can keep the rest of the meat to incorporate in other Chinese dishes or you can use it to make a wonderful brawn.

To do this shred the rest of the meat finely and chop up some of the skin into tiny pieces. Lay these in a shallow bowl and pour over enough of the cooking liquid to cover it. Put the bowl into the fridge and leave it overnight. The sauce will set into a wonderful jelly. Cut slices of the brawn to put into sandwiches or eat it with a salad and good bread.

Beef Stew with Sage

    4-6 ozs stewing beef
    $\frac{1}{2}$ small onion (peeled, chopped)
    1 dssrtspn olive oil
    1 dssrtspn plain flour
    6 whole fresh sage leaves
    2 fl ozs wine, cider or stock
    salt and freshly ground black pepper

Heat the oil in a frying pan and fry the onion in it until golden. Remove the onion to a casserole with a slotted spoon. Dust the meat, cut into 1-inch cubes, in the flour and fry in the oil until brown all over. Put the browned meat cubes into the casserole with a slotted spoon. Add the wine, cider or stock to the frying-pan and deglaze it, letting the liquid bubble for a few minutes to reduce the amount of liquid. Pour this sauce over the meat and onions in the casserole. Add six whole sage leaves (dried sage does not work), stir, cover tightly and either simmer it gently for $1\frac{1}{2}$ hours or cook in the oven for the same time at 170°C (325°F), Gas Mark 3. This can be prepared the day before you need it (up to the point where you put it into the oven), and kept in the fridge before being given its final long period of cooking. Serve with a good bread and a side salad.

Variation: Stewing pork, lamb or rabbit can be prepared in exactly the same way. With lamb and rabbit use two sprigs of fresh rosemary instead of sage. You can also add 1 tablespoon of finely chopped carrot and celery to the onions when they are frying. A baked potato is a good accompaniment. Mop up the sauce with bread.

Italian Fried Steak with Tomato Sauce

This is a simple way of enjoying "steak" without having to buy expensive cuts of T-bone, fillet or sirloin.

This is another of those dishes my son says that he would "kill for."

Eat simply with a side salad and a pitta bread, or slices of good bread, to dunk in the sauce.

> 4 ozs round steak (or rib)
> 3-4 stoned black olives
> 1 fl oz water
> $\frac{1}{2}$ medium onion (peeled)
> 3-4 fl ozs basic tomato sauce for pasta
>   (see "Pasta Recipes")

Wrap the meat in some cellophane or grease-proof paper and place it in the ice-making compartment of the fridge for about an hour. You are not trying to freeze it solid, only stiffen it enough to cut easily into thin slices across the grain.

While the meat is in the fridge prepare a basic tomato sauce as if you were going to eat pasta. You should add about twice the amount of onion recommended in that recipe. Alternatively you can use some of the basic sauce prepared in advance. If you are doing this then you should fry $\frac{1}{2}$ a medium-sized onion, sliced thinly, in a tablespoonful of olive oil and add it to the sauce. Now heat the sauce in a casserole and keep it hot in the oven. Add the olives chopped into small pieces. Take out the meat from the fridge and while it is still cold and stiff slice it, across the grain, into pieces no more than $\frac{1}{4}$ inch thick.

Take a dry frying-pan (the one in which the onions were cooked will do fine as long as you wipe out the oil with absorbent paper) and heat it up over a medium heat. You don't want it to burn but it should be very hot. Take about five or six of the thin slices of meat and lay them out flat in the pan. They should sizzle on contact. (If they do not do this the pan is not hot enough.) If it is hot enough then after 30 seconds beads of moisture will appear on the upper surface of the meat slices. Turn them over at once using a spatula or a kitchen tongs. Cook them on this side for another 20 seconds or so then lift them out and bury them in the hot tomato sauce. Cook all the meat this way. Now deglaze the pan with the water. Little bits of meat and a red sediment will have stuck to the bottom of the pan when you were cooking the meat. Use the spatula to detach these and mix them into the water which should bubble fiercely and reduce in volume. It will turn a rich, dark brown. Pour this sauce into the hot tomato sauce containing the meat and mix it in. Serve at once with a salad and bread.

Chicken Breast with Parsley and Lemon Sauce

A side of chicken breast costs no more in a supermarket than a lamb chop or a very small piece of steak. It cooks in a very few minutes and two of them (or one whole breast) will feed two people generously if cooked this way.

Serve with a salad, good bread and some tiny boiled new potatoes.

This is a useful, "planned" spur-of-the-moment dish to impress a friend of the opposite sex with your culinary prowess. (The planning needed is to have bought the chicken and the new potatoes. You should have the parsley and lemon juice in your emergency store cupboard.)

    1 chicken breast
    1 dssrtspn olive oil
    1 tsp butter
    1 tbs lemon juice
    1 tbs fresh chopped parsley
    1 tbs water
     ground black pepper

Remove the skin from the chicken breast. The breast will pull apart naturally into two pieces (one of which is bigger than the other). Slice the larger piece in two to give you three pieces roughly the same size.

Put your new potatoes on to boil. Heat the olive oil in a frying pan over a medium heat. Add half of the butter when the pan is hot and when the butter begins to foam put in the three chicken pieces. Cook them quickly on both sides. They will take about two minutes on each side and should be browned but not burnt. Check if they are cooked through by slicing into the thickest part of each fillet with a sharp knife (any juice should be absolutely clear with no trace of pinkness). When they are done remove them from the pan and keep them warm.

Lower the heat a little, and add the lemon juice and the water to the pan. Deglaze the pan with this, scraping up the little bits of meat and residue stuck to the bottom with a spatula. Let the sauce thicken a little and then add the parsley and the rest of the butter. Stir it round till the butter has melted then return the chicken to the pan to coat it in the sauce. Serve the chicken with the sauce from the pan poured over it.

Liver with Herbs and Mushrooms

Lamb's liver is the mildest in flavour but can be difficult to get fresh in small butchers' shops. Calf's liver is the next mildest in flavour but the shortage of veal in shops suggests that most of what is sold is not calf's liver at all. Pig's liver comes next in strength and ox or beef liver I find almost inedible it is so strong.

If you find the taste of liver too strong, try soaking it in milk overnight in the fridge. Wash it and dry it thoroughly when you take it out of the milk. If you know a friendly neighbourhood cat it will kill for the milk. If you strike up a relationship with your butcher ask him to slice the liver thinly for you. The quicker you can cook it, the better it tastes.

2-3 thin slices of liver (3-4 ozs)
1 dssrtspn olive oil
2-3 mushrooms
¼ small onion (peeled)
1 dssrtspn parsley or chives (chopped)
1 dssrtspn plain flour
salt and freshly ground black pepper
1 tsp lemon juice

Chop the mushrooms and the onion very finely and mix with the chopped parsley or chives. Heat the pan and add the oil. Let it heat until it is hot but not burning. Season the flour with the salt and black pepper and dust the slices of liver with this just before you put them into the pan. Brown them quickly on both sides. Now add the chopped mushroom, onion and parsley, turn down the heat and cook gently for 3 more minutes. Turn up the heat for a few seconds and add the lemon juice. Give everything a quick stir and serve at once.

Chicken Livers and Bacon

3-4 whole chicken livers
2 rashers of streaky bacon

I know people who "cannot bear" liver who quite happily eat this dish.

Chicken livers are often sold with the hearts still attached. (They look like tiny hearts, believe it or not, and are hard to the touch rather than soft like the liver.) Wash the livers and remove the hearts. (I would use them the next day, chopped very finely, to enrich a meat and tomato sauce for pasta.) Dry the livers thoroughly with absorbent kitchen paper and cut away any fat or green spots. This is quite normal. There is nothing wrong with the liver unless there is more green than purple coloured meat. Remove the rind from the bacon rashers and cut them in half. With the flat of a knife blade stretch each half of rasher until it is roughly twice its original length. Wrap each chicken liver in a piece of rasher. You can secure them with cocktail sticks if you think it is necessary. Grill them under a medium grill, turning them so that all of the rasher is crisp. By the time this is achieved the liver will be perfectly cooked. It will take about 5 minutes.

Chicken Livers with Ham

3 chicken livers
1 small slice of cooked ham
2 fl ozs chicken stock
1 dssrtspn chopped parsley
1 dssrtspn seasoned flour
1 dssrtspn olive oil

Prepare the livers as in the previous recipe and cut in two. Cut the ham into small squares. Heat the oil in a frying pan. Dust the livers in the seasoned flour and fry in the oil for two minutes turning them over at least once. Pour in the stock. (You could use wine if you had some.) Let the sauce bubble for 20 seconds then turn down the heat and simmer for four minutes, stirring it frequently.

Serve at once sprinkled with the chopped parsley. Plain boiled rice is a good accompaniment to this dish.

Lamb and Pork Kidneys

Cheap, quick to cook, and nutritionally almost as valuable as liver, kidneys tend to be a forgotten source of valuable nutrients. Many people are put off by the smell of kidneys when they are cooking, mistakenly believing that this comes from the residues left by their function in the body of the animal when it is alive. This is not true. One way of removing this smell is to cook the kidneys in milk or, at the very least, to soak them in milk before cooking. They are often sold still wrapped in a pale, almost transparent, skin which should be removed before you soak or cook them. It pulls off very easily. Cut the kidney in half lengthways and snip out the little root of dense white fat. The simplest way to cook them is to grill them. Brush them with oil and place under a pre-heated grill. Turn them frequently. They take only about 6-8 minutes depending on their thickness. They are better if still juicy and pink inside.

Variation: Fry the kidneys (sliced in half lengthways,) in a pan just smeared with oil. You can burn them on the outside but do not let them dry out. Then pour 2 fluid ounces of cream into the pan to deglaze it and boil rapidly to reduce the sauce. Serve the kidneys with this sauce poured over them.

For devilled kidneys fry a small onion, which has been chopped very finely, in a tablespoonful of olive oil until it is beginning to brown. Add the kidneys cut into $\frac{1}{4}$ inch thick slices. Stir and fry fiercely for 2 minutes then add 1 fluid ounce of cream, 1 tablespoonful of Lea & Perrins Worcester Sauce, 1 teaspoon of Dijon mustard, 3 twists of ground black pepper, a handful of fresh chopped parsley, and a small pinch of cayenne pepper. Boil it all up rapidly to reduce and thicken the sauce (2 minutes) then serve with plain boiled rice.

Pork Chops

Pork chops were once one of my favourite foods. They were also, and still are, substantially cheaper than lamb or beef. Today, because of the breeding of lean pigs and the handling of the animals before slaughter, pork can be very unreliable. This has nothing to do with disease or hormones. Pigs are extremely excitable and nervous animals. When they become nervous or over-excited they produce massive amounts of adrenalin which chemically affects their meat. When the animals are killed in this distressed state the meat which results is described as "stressed." It seems to me that much of the pork sold today is "stressed" and that is more of a comment on the way the animals are handled prior to slaughter than on the way they are actually killed. The result is pork meat which is tough, leathery and often "grey and watery" looking even before it is cooked.

Not all pork is like this. But unless you can be sure of your source (remember what I said about making friends with your butcher), then I'm going to recommend that you adopt a careful strategy when cooking pork chops.

1 pork chop
1 tbs olive oil
1 tsp butter
1 dssrtspn seasoned flour
1 dssrtspn chopped tomato
1 clove garlic (peeled, chopped)
1 tsp fresh chopped sage leaves
2 fl ozs cider, wine or water

Heat the oil and butter in a frying-pan over a medium heat. Dry the chop and add it to the pan (along with the chopped garlic) to brown quickly on both sides. (2 minutes per side.) Add the tomato, sage and cider and season with salt and freshly ground black pepper. Allow this liquid to bubble up for 30 seconds then cover the pan tightly and turn down the heat to very low. Cook for about 1 hour. This can be done in the oven as well. (140°C, 275°F, Gas Mark 1)

Remove the chop to a hot plate, add 2 tablespoons of water and stir up the sauce to loosen any residues stuck to the pan. Turn up the heat and boil the sauce fiercely to reduce it slightly. Pour over the chop and serve sprinkled with the chopped parsley.

Indian Style Pork Sausages

$\frac{1}{2}$ inch cube of fresh ginger root (peeled and finely chopped)
1 large clove garlic (peeled, crushed and chopped)
1 tbs water
1 small courgette (quartered lengthways)
1 dssrtspn vegetable or olive oil
3 pork sausages
1 small onion (peeled, chopped)
$\frac{1}{3}$ tsp ground cumin seeds
small pinch cayenne pepper (optional)
2 tomatoes (tinned Italian plum, chopped)
pinch salt

Make a paste of the garlic, water and fresh ginger root with your mortar and pestle. If you don't have fresh ginger root then substitute 1/3 teaspoon of dried ground ginger. Fresh ginger root is used in many Indian dishes (if you are feeling adventurous) and keeps well in the fridge for quite long periods.

Heat the oil on your frying-pan over a medium flame and fry the sausages, turning them until they are brown on all sides. Remove the sausages from the pan and keep them on a plate.

Put the onion into the same pan and fry them until they begin to brown at the edges. Now add the garlic and ginger paste to the pan. Stir it through the onions and fry for 2 minutes. Add the crushed cumin seeds and the cayenne if you are using it. Stir. Add the tomatoes and stir them while they fry for 2 minutes. Add the courgette quarters (cut into 1 inch lengths) and a pinch of salt. Bring the contents of the pan to a simmer, cover the pan and turn the heat to low. Let it cook for 10 minutes. Cut the sausages into bite-sized pieces. Add them to the pan and cook, covered, for another 5 minutes or until the sausages have heated through.

Serve with either boiled rice or with the potatoes and black pepper on page 120.

Chilli con Carne

This is a perfect and economical dish for serving at a party—it can be prepared in advance and can be reheated in the oven. Serve it with lots of garlic bread and dressed green salad. The quantities are for about 10-12 people. It is not a dish I would recommend that you prepare just for yourself but if you want to try it just divide the quantities in this recipe by eight.

    2 lb of lean mince
    24 ozs dried or 2 (16 oz) tins red kidney beans
    4 onions peeled and chopped
    4 tbs olive oil
    2 tins (16 oz) Italian plum tomatoes
    3 tsp chilli seasoning (not cayenne pepper)
    1 handful of chopped, fresh parsley
    1 fresh green chilli pepper (optional)
    salt and freshly ground black pepper (to taste)

If you are using dried red kidney beans, wash them carefully and leave them to soak overnight in cold water. I would recommend that you save yourself a lot of trouble by using tinned, cooked beans. Sharwoods have a particularly good tinned variety which are relatively inexpensive. This way the beans need only to be added for the final stages of cooking so that they are heated thoroughly. If you are using dried beans you should bring them to the boil, boil them hard for 10-15 minutes, then turn down the heat and simmer them until they are cooked tender. Depending on the beans this will take from 1-2 hours. When they are cooked, drain them and cool them in cold water. When they are cold, drain them thoroughly and set them aside until you need to add them to the minced meat mixture.

I have to warn you here about the difference between chilli pepper (ground cayenne pepper) which is a bright orangey red colour (and "brutally" hot) and chilli seasoning. The latter which is what you need for this recipe, is a dark, browny-red powder. It is usually sold in small jars or cartons in the spice racks of supermarkets. It is, in fact, a mixture of ground herbs and spices (with some cayenne pepper included) but is not nearly as hot as chilli pepper. The jar or packet will always give a list of the ingredients so if you are in any doubt about which you are buying check this list. Chilli pepper will only contain ground cayenne pepper. Chilli seasoning will have a number of other ingredients like oregano, cumin, garlic and others along with some cayenne. A good rule of thumb is that the darker brown the seasoning is in the jar the less likely it is to be too "hot." Where a manufacturer offers a seasoning in different strengths (usually "mild," "medium" or "hot") then buy the mildest. You may sometimes come across names like "Mexican" seasoning as well. But those suitable for making this dish will usually say something like suitable for Chilli con Carne somewhere on the label.

Heat the oil in a large, oven proof pot or casserole, over a low heat. When it is hot add the chopped onions and fry them gently until they are soft and golden. Now add the minced beef and fry it. You must stir it and break it up constantly with a wooden spoon to make sure that all of it is cooked. When it is cooked thoroughly it will have broken up into fine grains of meat rather than the lumps you started with. Now add the chilli seasoning. If you are unsure of how hot the powder might be then add just two gently rounded teaspoonfuls. Mix it through the mince and onions with your wooden spoon and continue to fry the mixture gently for another five minutes. This is the point at which you add the whole fresh chilli pepper if you are going to. To do this, split it lengthways with a sharp knife. Remove every single one of the tiny white seeds and throw them away. Cut off the stem of the chilli and then slice the flesh into thin slivers and add to the pot.

Open the two tins of tomatoes and strain off the excess water or juice. Add these to the pot and break up the tomatoes while you are stirring them through the meat. Turn up the heat until the sauce in the pot is bubbling then turn down the heat to low, season it with salt and pepper, add the chopped parsley, cover the pot and simmer it gently for about 2 hours. Check it often to see that it is not drying out. If it seems too dry then add a little water. Now add the cooked beans and mix them through the meat sauce gently, trying not to break them up in the process. If you are serving the dish at once, cook it for another twenty minutes or so until the beans are hot through. If you are preparing it in advance, add the beans and mix them through but do not continue the cooking at this point. You will need to put the pot, covered, into a preheated, moderate oven for about forty minutes to heat it up before serving it.

One point to watch out for if you are using tinned beans: wash away the sauce or juice which comes in the tin. It is usually too sweet and even if it is not, adding extra liquid at this point can make the sauce too watery. It should have a thick, slightly oily, dryish consistency and not be at all soupy. Serve with good, fresh bread (or with the hot garlic bread for which I give the recipe below) and lots of dressed green salad.

Hot Garlic Bread

2 loaves of bread (either French sticks or Vienna rolls)
6 oz softened butter
3 large cloves of garlic (peeled, finely chopped)
2 tbs fresh, finely chopped parsley
a little salt and freshly ground black pepper
aluminium cooking foil (enough to wrap around the loaves)

You must use real butter for this recipe, you cannot use any low-fat dairy spread or margarine for this recipe because they give an oily, unpleasant flavour.

Take a piece of foil large enough to completely cover the bread when wrapped round it. Slice the bread into thick (1 inch) slices. Do not cut right through the bread. It should remain joined together at the bottom of each slice.

Peel and chop the garlic very finely. Sprinkle a little salt and pepper onto a flat surface and crush the garlic with the flat of a knife to form a paste. Add this paste to the softened butter and mix it thoroughly. If you are using parsley then add this to the butter as well at this point.

Spread this butter, thinly on both sides of each slice of the bread. Wrap up the bread in the foil. Prepare the second loaf in the same way. Bake the bread in the foil in a pre-heated, moderate to medium oven 190°C (375°F) Gas Mark 5 for 15-20 minutes. Open up the foil for the last 5 minutes to allow the bread to crisp. Serve it piping hot. If you are serving this with Chilli con Carne you can cook the bread, for the final 20 minutes, in the same oven that you are using to re-heat the Chilli.

Rouxes, Veloutés, Sauces and Dressings

There are more myths encouraged by professional chefs about the subject of this chapter than about any other single topic in the craft of cooking. The processes are basically simple and, as long as you exercise care, no more care than you would apply to any task which takes a modicum of concentration, anyone can achieve the required result.

Basic White Sauce or Roux

You cannot make tiny amounts of this. Make more than you need and either throw the surplus away or store it in the fridge. If you do that you can either use it a within a couple of days or throw it away then.

> 2 dssrtspns plain white flour
> 2 dssrtspns melted butter
> 5 fl ozs milk
> salt and freshly ground black pepper

Melt the butter in a small saucepan, when it foams, stir in the flour and cook it over a low heat, stirring all the time, until it is blended. Do not let it colour or brown. Remove it from the heat and let it stand for 2 minutes. This is a roux. Pour in all of the milk at once, whisking vigorously. Put it back over a moderate heat and bring it to the boil, whisking gently all the time. Allow it to boil up for just a moment or two then take it off the heat, season it and give it a final whisk. This is a basic white sauce.

Variations: As soon as the milk has boiled up take it off the heat and add 1 tablespoonful of grated cheese, either cheddar or a hard "grana" type. This is a basic cheese sauce.

Instead of cheese add 2 tablespoonsful of fresh finely chopped parsley. This is a basic parsley sauce.

Add 1 tablespoonful of chopped mushrooms as soon as the milk boils. This is a basic mushroom sauce.

Velouté Sauce

A Velouté is made in exactly the same way as a basic white sauce but using chicken, meat, fish or vegetable stock instead of milk. It is usual to allow the roux to colour slightly before removing it from the heat to add the stock.

If you have no stock then you can use a stock or bouillon cube. Do remember that 1 stock cube makes $\frac{3}{4}$ of a pint of stock so you need only use $\frac{1}{3}$ of a cube for your velouté. Stock cubes contain massive amounts of salt so do not add any seasoning.

Variation: Add 1 dessertspoonful of tomato paste or 1 tablespoon of chopped tomato. This will give the sauce a pinkish tinge and a slightly tomato-ish taste which some people like with fish.

Gravy

Gravy can divide families into opposing camps. Some people are addicted to the kind that is browned, thickened and seasoned all in one go! I prefer a thinner gravy which tastes of the meat I am serving. A compromise gravy which is acceptable to most reasonable people follows.

> 1 tbs of the fat from the meat being roasted.
> 1 tbs plain flour
> 8 fl ozs. stock or
> 1 Oxo cube dissolved in 8 fl ozs boiling water

Pour off all of the fat which gathers in the roasting tin when the meat is cooked except for 1 tablespoonful. Put the tin on top of the cooker over a low heat. Sprinkle on the flour and stir it into the fat. Let it cook for a moment or two. It will begin to brown. Pour in the stock or Oxo. Stir and whisk vigorously to scrape up all the meat deposits in the bottom of the roasting tin. Keep cooking and whisking until it thickens. This will take about 3 minutes. Serve in a heated jug.

Apple Sauce

> 1 Bramley cooking apple
> 1 tsp butter
> 1-2 tsp sugar
> 1 dssrtspn water

Peel, core and chop up the flesh of the apple. Put this in a small pot with the water. Cook over a moderate heat until it softens and fluffs. (Only a Bramley apple will do this properly.) Add the butter and the sugar and stir it in well. Taste it. You may need a little more sugar for your taste. I also add a little ground black pepper.

Mayonnaise

Even a good commercial mayonnaise like Hellmann's bears about as much relation to the taste of real, home-made mayonnaise as stock cubes do to good home-made stock. To make your own mayonnaise you need patience and elbow-grease.

> 1 egg yolk
> 6-8 fl ozs oil
> 1 dssrtspn lemon juice (or wine vinegar)

All of these ingredients must be at room temperature so if they have been stored in a fridge let them warm up for half-an-hour. Separate the yolk from the white of an egg. (Store the white in the fridge and use it later to add to an omelette or to bind the meat mixture for a hamburger or meatballs.) Put the yolk into the bottom of a bowl. Stand the bowl on a damp cloth on the work surface to prevent it sliding around when you are mixing the mayonnaise.

Mayonnaise changes its flavour and consistency depending on the quality of the oil with which it is made. A really good, green, fruity, virgin olive oil is incomparable for taste but can be a little overpowering (and rather expensive). A compromise is a half-and-half mixture of good olive oil and a sunflower oil.

Put the oil into a measuring jug with a pouring-lip. Whisk the egg yolk with a pinch of salt and a twist of ground black pepper. (You might add $\frac{1}{2}$ teaspoon of Dijon mustard at this point but it is not necessary.) Using a wooden spoon stir the egg while adding drops of oil from the jug. You really must add it in small drops to start with and stir them in well before adding the next. As it gets thicker you can add the oil in a thin continuous stream. You must stir continuously. Stop adding oil and when the last drop of oil you added is fully incorporated take a rest. You will need to have added about $\frac{1}{3}$ of the oil before you can begin to add it in a thin stream. After a rest add a small amount of the lemon juice or vinegar and mix it in well before you add the next drop of oil.

When all the oil is incorporated you will have a thick, fluffy mayonnaise. Taste it, adjust the seasoning and add the remains of the lemon juice or wine vinegar. This "sets" the mayonnaise.

If at any stage the mixture "curdles" on you (it will look oily and grainy) then do not panic. Take another yolk of egg in a separate bowl and begin again, adding the curdled mixture to the new egg drop by drop.

If you know that you will not be eating all of this mayonnaise at once then stir in 1 dessertspoonful of boiling water before putting it away in the least cold section of the fridge.

Variation : Aïoli is a mayonnaise with added garlic. Simply add a paste (made in your mortar and pestle with two small crushed cloves of garlic, a pinch of salt and 2 drops of oil) to the egg yolk before you start mixing in the oil.

Yoghurt-based Dressings

If you like yoghurt then a good-quality, plain, un-sweetened (preferably "live") yoghurt can be used instead of mayonnaise as the basis for a dressing with some dishes. It has a much sharper, tangier taste than mayonnaise but if it is too strong for you and you find mayonnaise too rich then a mixture of yoghurt and mayonnaise might be just what you are looking for.

Take a carton of plain unsweetened yoghurt. If you can find one labeled "live" or "unpasteurised" they taste much better. These are sometimes labeled Bulgarian Yoghurt. Don't shake the carton. Pour off any of the colourless liquid that might have gathered on top. Now stir in salt and freshly ground black pepper. Taste it until it is right for your taste. Now you can add chopped herbs just as you might with mayonnaise or mix in a teaspoon of lemon juice. Experiment until you find a flavour that suits you.

Index